Scottish

Thoughts and Reflections

Vol 21

With Colour Photographs

The Twenty-First in a series since moving back to Scotland from South Africa in August 2018.

David R B Nicoll

Meet you! With love! David! xxx

D... Dec'24

David was inducted as an International Poet of Merit with the International Society of Poetry in America in 1997 and made it to the semi-finals of a poetry competition there between 2000 selected poets from all over the world. He has had poetry published in South African and International magazines and newspapers and was listed in the International Who's Who of Poetry in 2012. He has released quite a number of poetry books, lots with matching photographs, also POKE POetic joKE books some with illustrations and Tattoo/Body Art books. He has also released CDs with poetry and music. All CDs to date recorded and produced in South Africa. Please check out his website with links to the books and CDs on www.davidnicoll.co.uk The CDs are also on YouTube!

There have been lyric videos made from some select tracks which are also on the website as well as a performance videos by others section which is great performances by fellow Poets and Musicians in the days BC!*

*=Before Corona!

Well, they were there until YouTube closed my channel that is!

Now Thehardbard on Bitchute and load my videos on Vimeo!

I would ask that no one take offence on any of the contents of this book, rather take it with a sense of humour!

We care about the planet and all life forms on it, we also object to many planes leaving long white streaks all over our skies and blocking out our sunshine amongst other things. Please join us if you do as well.

Face book groups:

SMAAPP Scottish Musicians and Artistes Against the Poisoning of our Planet

And

Anti Geoengineering Scotland.

Previous publications:

All available on Amazon as Paperback, Black and White or Colour Photographs? Also Kindle versions and some Hard Cover editions.

Readers Choice Edition Vol 1

Scottish Thoughts and Reflections Vol 1- 20!

Select Poetry from 2019-2021 Vol 1 and 2!

Tenerife Thoughts and Reflections Vol 1, Vol 2 Part 1 and 2!

Thoughts and Reflections Vols 1, 2 and 3.

The Poetic Picture book Vols 1 and 2.

POKEs POetic joKEs

This is POKES 2, 3, 4, 5 and 6 !

South African Tattoos

Northern Hemisphere Body Art/Tattoos Vol 1 and 2

A Case for Humanity Vol 1 and 2!

All links on www.davidnicoll.co.uk

And on my Amazon Author page.

If you enjoy the book,

Please do a review!

On Amazon,

Facebook,

Or any other

Platforms?

Thank you!

CDs all on YouTube and Spotify:

David Nicoll and friends Vols 1,2 and 3

With great thanks to the many friends and musicians who contributed

To the making of these CDs through my many wonderful years in South Africa.

With love to you all Soul Brothers and Sisters.

In collaboration with

Great thanks to Mervyn Fuller and friends for his musical creations.

Created in Gaansbai, Cape Town, South Africa.

I was the lyricist in the band known as MAD,

Mervyn and Myself became freinds a number of years ago, he was a retired singer Songwriter who used to play the music circuits in South Africa.

We lived a long way apart and every now and again he would phone me and say,

Write something about this! Then he would give me an idea which would spark me,

Would then write down the lyrics and send them to him. He would then decide

What type of song to make it, Rock, Reggae, Easy listening? Then put it together

And pull his friends Mike Pregnolatu to add lead Guitar and Mike Laatz on Saxophone.

The idea behind the MAD CDs is for you to listen to tracks

Where you resonate with the track titles. Some great original sounds and potent poetry.

Mervyn And Dave: Listed as Mervyn Fuller and David Nicoll on YouTube.

CDs

Treat it so!

This is MAD 2!

On Days like These!

The Best of MAD!

The Beat Goes On!

On the Home Straight!

Richard Doiron

Dec 30, 2023,
5:40 PM (1 day
ago)

Foreword for Scottish Thoughts and Reflections Vol 21

David Nicoll is a man of great - and varied - passions. He is extremely concerned about the declining state of the environment, something he easily attributes to ongoing, and destructive, programs, chief among those being geoengineering,

Which is the deliberate manipulation of our environment, our weather, in effect, the very web of life onto which we all cling.

David is a man who has travelled extensively, living on numerous continents. Born in Scotland, which he left for a long period, the man who "likes to build" structures and things, returned to his roots after being laid off from work. In some ways, moving back to his country of birth, specifically Glasgow, he was horrified to see how the skies of the city were being covered over by streams emitted by jet planes. He had seen this in far away lands, but seeing this replicated at home, prompted him to do something to inform as many people as possible on what was causing planes to leave such horrors behind.

A consummate musician, long involved in the field, producing albums with other musicians of note, for his part he would write lyrics to songs. And it somehow occurred to him that he was actually a poet; wanting to reach as many people as possible, he compiled books of poetry, wherein he identified many of the horrors of our time, from geoengineering to government corruption, to a medical establishment which was anything but.

I met David online some years ago and have been amazed at his energy, insights, and decidedly authentic activism. He is a man to be admired for his courage, for his in-depth research into what can only be seen as destructive elements in society, and for daring to speak his truths, without halt or hesitation. His ability to weave his overall observations into poetic works is rather astounding.

Meanwhile, here is a man who knows that telling the truth does not make a person popular in some circles, having had his Youtube channel shut down completely, for example. He knows that some social sectors are connected to other sectors and to expose one corrupt sector would ultimately tend to expose others equally corrupt, but David is not someone to give up on vital causes. He knows the fight to educate others will never be easy, with so many people having been conditioned to respond only to official narratives, oblivious to what should otherwise be plain to see, chemtrails being such things. But giving up is not an option for this man. He is both a man of the world and of the natural world, and that sets him apart from a great many, as he is able to connect the proverbial dots, as it were, and articulate things into fair conclusions.

I personally endorse David Nicoll and his ongoing efforts to enlighten the sleeping masses, as he strives to expose the destructive elements in our world, in a relentless pursuit of justice for all.

For ages, it has been said that the pen is mightier than the sword; David Nicoll's pen has long spilled voluminous amounts of ink in a most noble fashion. As a poet, he has a sensitive soul; as an activist he has the heart of a lion. The merging of both of those aspects makes all the difference in the world.

-Richard Doiron, poet

www.RicharDoiron.com

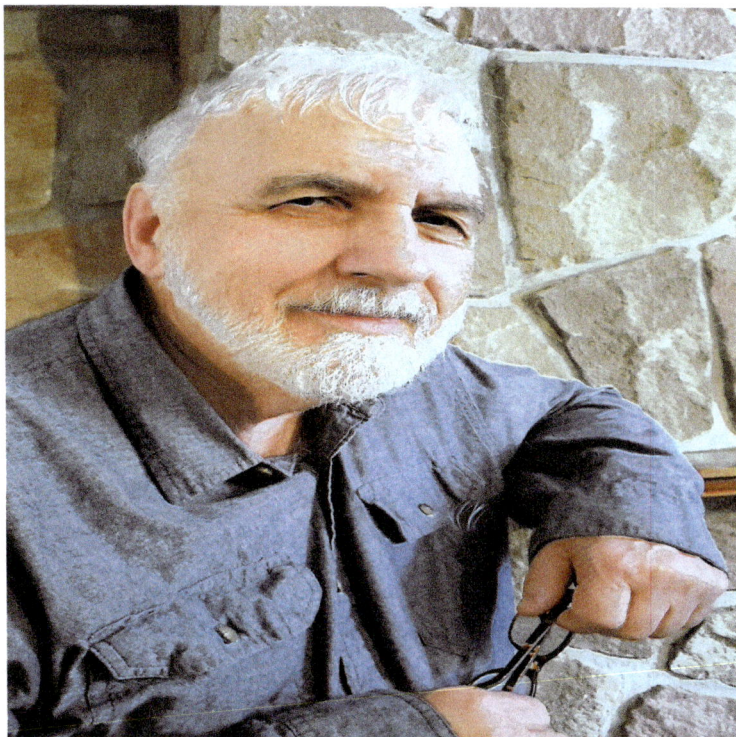

Index:

Comments on the poem titled To See!

Commodity!

Connection!*

Conspiracy!

Constantly!

Constipated!*

Control of Humanity!

Cough!*

Currently!*

Dance Choreographers Required!*

Dark Eventually!

Dave Caird!*

Day's!

Degree's!

Dick?*

Did You?*

Died!

Do!

Do I!

Doc McLean!*

Don't Hate!*

Easily!

Enough!

Even on Me?

Every Day!

Exactly!

Fairy!

Fall!

Fear!*

First!*

Flag's!

For Sure!*

Formation!*

Free!

Freezing!*

From Me!

Gates!

Gay!*

Geoengineered Insanity!*

Globally!*

Global Tyranny!

Glory Be!*

Gone Away!*

Grey!*

Guilty!*

Handy!

Head!*

Hi Neale!

Hidden Away!

His Last Trip!*

Holly!*

I Replied!

Immediately!

In 1954!

Inbox!

Instead!

Irish Border!*

Is Happy!

Is Tae Me!*

It Again!

It!

Ity!

Jokingly!*

Jubilee!

Just Wait and See!*

Kidding!

Knee!

Know!*

Land One Day!*

Later!

Laughter to You!*

Longer Away!*

Love!

Meant Happy!*

Meeeeee!!!!!"

Mercy!

Military!

Mind!*

Money!*

My Poetry!

Name Something!*

2030!

This
Morning,
I
Went
Downstairs,
For a
Smoke
And to
Welcome,
The new
Day!
Look up
And there
In the sky,
Is a
Long
White
Spray!
Unseen
By the
Majority,
Who are
So used,
To seeing
Them now,
That it is
Accepted,
As
Normality!
But this
Is not
The way,
That it
Used to
Be!
Of course
They are
Brainwashed,
Programmed
And
Hypnotised,

By their
Own
TV!
"They are
CONtrails
Only!"
They all
Agree!
Anyone
Who says
Anything
Different,
They call
A
"Theorist
In
Conspiracy!"
To
Ridicule
Them,
Unsuccessfully!
As we,
Can see,
The
Geoengineering
Programmes,
That are
Underway,
Currently!
And
Globally!
Alzheimer's
And
Dementia
Rates,
Rising
Stratospherically!
Due to a
Coagulation of
Aluminium,
In the
Brain,
Where it
Should not,

Be!
How it
Got there?
No doctors
Can agree!
Although it
Is listed as
A component,
In the
Sprays,
In nano
Particle
Form,
Duck Duck Go
The
Geoengineering
Patents
And there,
You will
See!
There are over
One hundred and
Sixty!
They are a
Threat to
Our whole
Environment
And
Humanity!
Poisoning
The
Air,
Land,
Rivers
And
Sea!
Spreading to
Block out
The
Sun!
Depriving us,
Of
Making
Vitamin D!

Cutting down
On
Photosynthesis,
Needed for
Growth,
In every
Living plant,
Vegetable and
Tree!
To sum it up
In one word,
It would be,
Insanity!
Funded by
The world's
Most famous
Doctor,
Without a
Medical
Degree!
Most known
For his
Philanthropy!
And
Promoting
Injections,
To
Supposedly,
Prevent you
Catching
C_V_D!
With
Eugenistic
Traits,
From his
Family!
Much less
People,
On this
Beautiful
Planet,
They
Would like
To see!

Check out
The
Now
Demolished,
Georgia
Guidestones,
Carved
Inscriptions,
Their
Intention,
Is stated
Clearly!
The world
Now being
Run by
Many an
Unelected,
Body!
The
WEF,
WHO,
EU
And
UN!
With
Depopulation
Plans,
Including
Agenda
2030!

A for Away!

Just had a
Lovely meal
With my family,
Who gave me
The most
Beautiful
Rose,
That I
Ever
Did
See!
The
Rainbow
Rose,
It should
Be called,
Obviously!
Thank you
Also for
The other
Great
Birthday
Gifts,
They
Know
That I
Love,
Being
Alive!
One
Being an
Anywhere?
Anytime?
Free
Fall
Skydive!

To Papa Africa/Tenerise

You are Going
SKYDIVING

Have a Wonderful
Birthday

Lots of Love from ALL of US

XXX (so excited to go away
with you♡
Love from Hope xxx

Thank you all for a

Wonderful

Seventieth

Birthday,

I must

Say!

As for the

Brilliant

Present,

It is,

"A

For Away!"   With Love XXX

A Literary Minefield!

You have to be careful

How you spell things now

Apparently!

Especially,

When using words

Like Vaxxines,

Or C_V_D?

As the AI and

Algorithms,

Would pick them up,

Easily!

You are not allowed

To expose any Truth,

Regarding either

Of them,

You see!

Exposing

Skullduggery,

By those

In authority,

Who have currently,

Got an ongoing,

Culling of Humanity!

Study,

The increase in

Overall death statistics,

Globally,

That can be

Seen

Easily!

Geoengineering,

Cutting down

On the,

Agricultural yield!

Living in day's of a

Literary,

Minefield!

A Neat Touch!

A Review!

Met a lady
Outside the
727 Chippy
Near Oran mor
Last Saturday night,
It was after
Two in the morning,
There was a long
Queue going
Right out
The door,
But we were
Both feeling
Alright,
Talking about how
Great the Glasgow
Social scene is,
Regardless
Of where
You roam,
The live band's
The social scene,
The people
At home!
"It's a pity
That there is
Such a queue!"
"Not to worry!"
I said.
"I get
Preferential
Treatment here
And know,
What to do!
What would
You like?
OK then,
A fish supper
For you!"
Upon getting
Inside the door

And into view,
After a nod,
My usual
Half pizza
And chips
Was being
Prepared
"Please add on
Another
Fish and chips
Too!"
Paid for them,
Then gave them a copy
Of my latest book,
Tenerife Thought's
And Reflections Vol 2!
Then asked
"Could you
Please,
Write a
Review?"

A Sign of the Times!

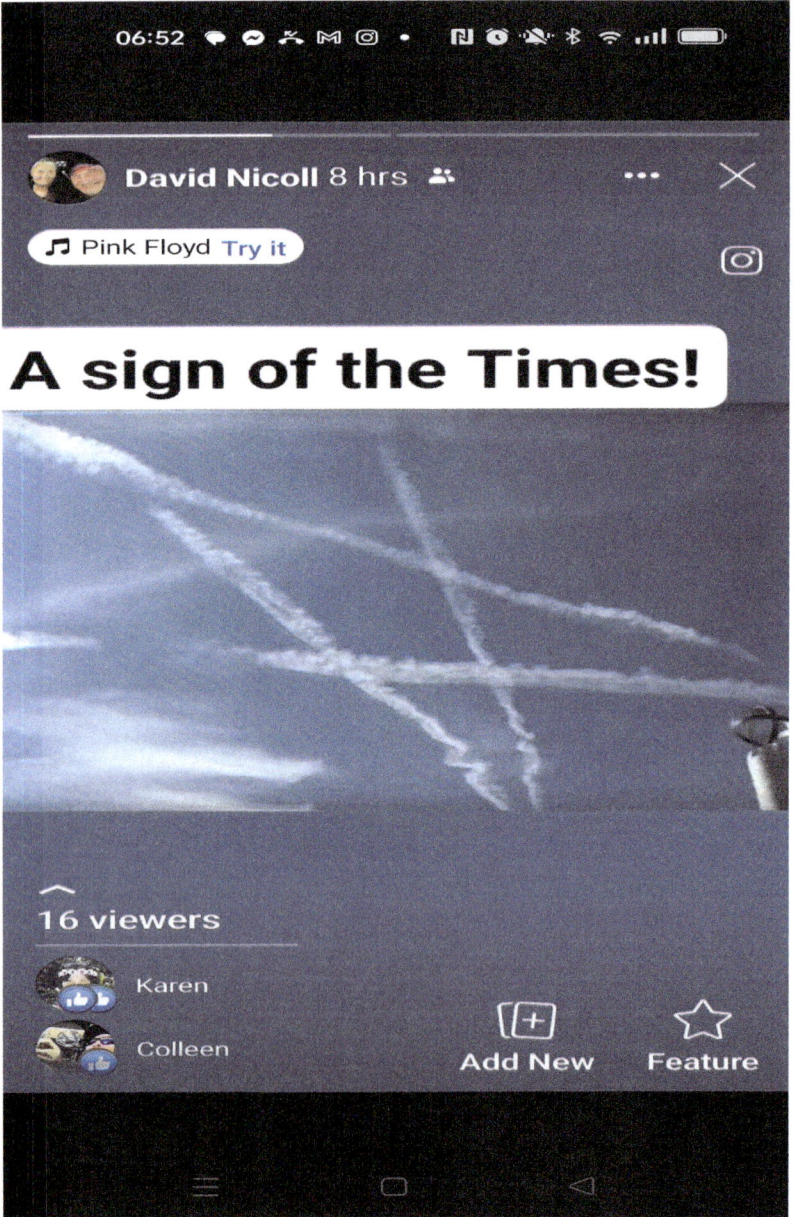

Accommodation!

Wull Boyle:
Soon be no Armies or police forces....so the primed an ready UN WHO WEF "Migrants" soldiers can Descend on us.

David:

They are
Ready and
Waiting,
In this very
Nation!
Illegal
Immigrants,
Now
Called
(Asylum
Seekers)
Currently
Being
Put
Up
For
Free,
In
Four Star,
Accommodation!

While the

British homeless

Sleep on the street!

What is going on?

Is a

Move!

Showing the

Empires

Retreat!

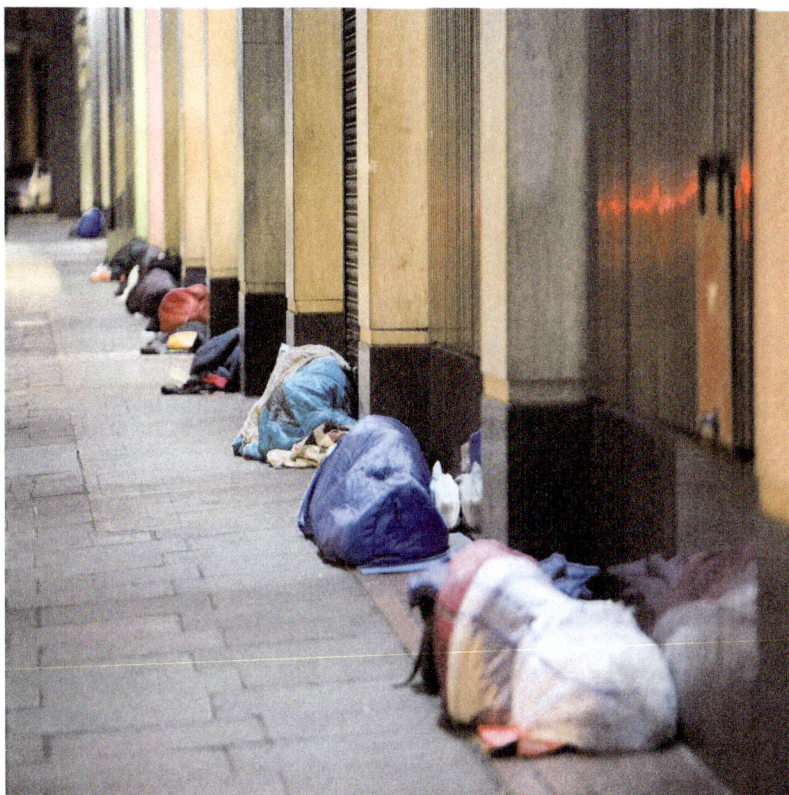

AD!

Mona Amberland:
What is your Clan?

David:
I come from the
Clan Macleod!
Got referred to as
MacLeod of
MacLeod the Seer!
Many years ago in
Washington DC!
Attending an International
Symposium of Poetry,
The gave an
International Poet of Merit,
Beautiful medallion to me!
MacLeod,
Means Son of Leod!
As we are from the
Outer Hebrides you see!
Which were ruled by the
Kingdom of Norway from
800 to 1200 AD!

Adeje!

It's much
Better
Down here,
Than
Scotland,
Sunshine
Again!
Very little
Strain!
Everyone
Happy!
On
Holiday,
From the
World's troubles ,
Very far
Away!
Following the
Mantra of
"Live For
Today!"
Greatful for the
Serendipity,
Still busy,
Writing
Books
Of
Poetry!
That brought
Me to the
Tenerife,
Beautiful
Volcanic
Island,
To
Stay,
In
Costa,
Adeje!

© SPL / Barcroft Media

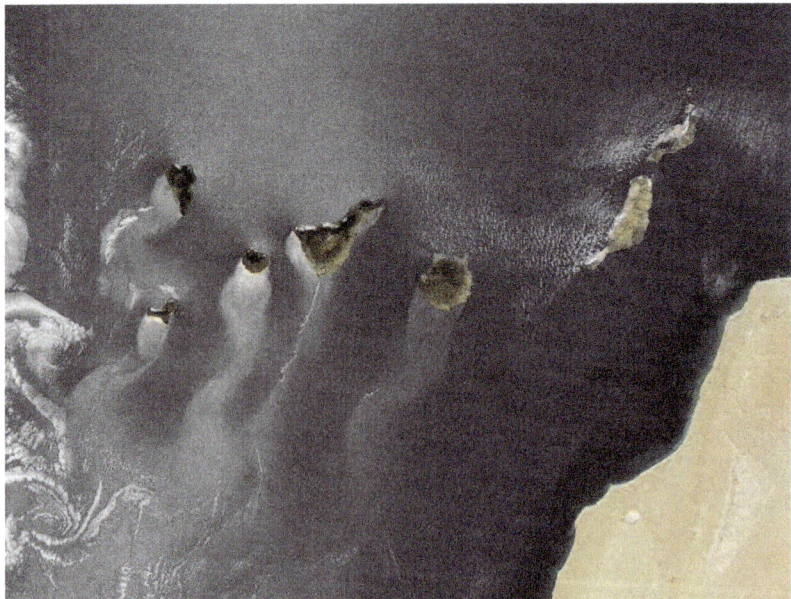

Again!

Looking
At the
Photo
Of your
Beautiful
Lips,
Brought
Back
A
Fond
Memory!
Of us
Being
On a
Secluded
Park bench,
Beneath an
Overhanging,
Shady
Tree!
I am now
Living in
Scotland,
Land of
Protest
And
Imposed,
Strain!
Would
Be,
Lovely,
To
Do it,
Again!

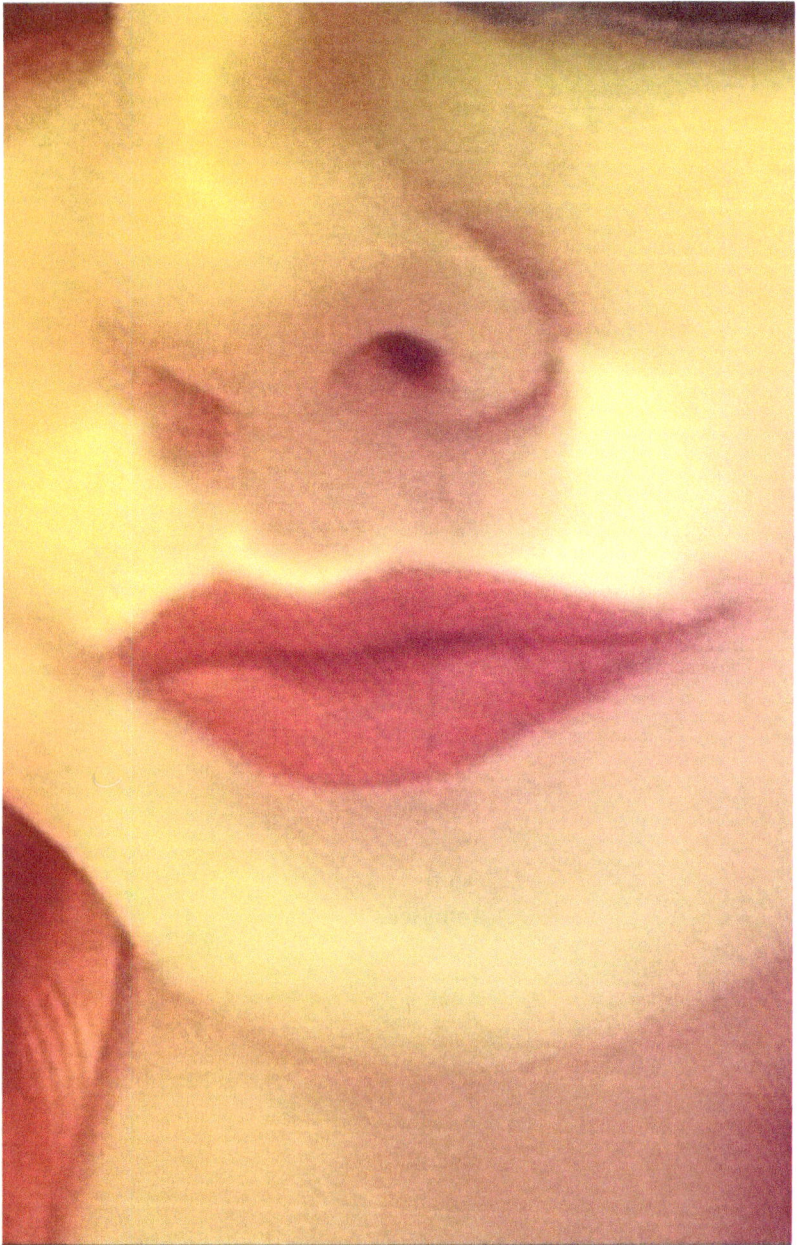

Agree!

There is a
Culling of Humanity,
Ongoing today!
It takes many forms
So to say!
One example being
The Toxic metallic
Nano particles
That into
Our skies,
They Spray!
Every day!
Most have eyes
But cannot see!
Because they
Are Hypnotised,
Programmed and
Bamboozled,
By their
Own TV!
"They are
CONtrails,
Only!"
They all
Agree!
Unfortunately!
"Duck Duck Go,"
Geoengineering
And you
Will see!
A global
Pandemic,
Arranged
And
Orchestrated,
Recently!
Against an
Invisible virus,
Known as
C_V_D!
With a

Ninety nine percent
Chance even if
You catch it,
Of
Recovery!
But then
Unauthorized,
Experimental,
So called
Vaxxines,
Were rolled out
Urgently!
Their,
Uptake,
Being
Mandatory!
Now
Millions
Are dead,
In a
Crematorium?
Or
Cemetery?
With millions
More afflicted,
Heavily!
With no
Recourse or
Help from those,
In Authority!
To be eligible
To get the
120 thousand pound
Payout,
In percentage points,
You have
To be,
Debilitated,
By a
Percentage,
Of
Sixty!
The Vaxx makers,
With Zero,

Liability!
Them profiting
Grotesquely!
As well as
Oor Bill!
Who invested
In the seven main
Vaxx makers,
Also sold his shares
In Fixer,
Profiting
Astronomically!
Before their
Drop in
Profits,
Coincidentally?
Chasing Elon,
He doesn't like
Being in the
World's Richest Man table,
Behind Jeff and Elon,
At Number Three!
Profiting,
Stratospherically!
In an ongoing
Genocide!
Just waiting for
The WHO,
To declare
The next
PLANNEDemic,
Emergency!
With powers to
Declare
Lock Downs,
Anytime,
Anywhere!
Soon no country,
Will be left with,
With any
National,
Sovereignty!
Bill also
Funds them,

Purely
Coincidentally!
Undoubtedly!
The jabs also
Create,
Sterility
A lot
Less people,
On this
Beautiful
Jewel,
Of a
Planet,
The
Eugenists,
Greedy and
Power
Hungry!
Would like
To see!
Not less
Of them,
But a
LOT less of
You and Me!
Not so
Many,
Now in
Maaui!
Where residents
Had no access
To water,
To fight the fires,
No electricity!
Denied to
Leave the town,
By those in
Authority!
They fried
In their cars,
No trace of
Them left,
For anyone
To see!

A land
Clearance,
Possibly?
Word has it that
The Powers
That be!
Want to
Turn the
Whole island,
Into a
SMART
City!
Run by
AI,
Apparently!
Well, Well,
Time will tell,
And we
Shall
See!
Many thousands
Already,
Now in the
Cold ground,
In the war,
Fought by
Proxy!
Making the
Arms
Suppliers,
Very
Happy!
They need
War!
Constantly!
Now what do
We see?
An armed
Incursion
By a
Terrorist,
(Freedom
Fighter)
Group,

Apparently!
Who drove out
Of the worlds
Largest,
Open air,
Concentration
Camp!
In many,
A brand new
Looking,
White
SUV!
"Where dId
They come from?"
Is a question,
That came
To me!
Then
Armed
Paratroopers,
Floating down
Silently!
Whose plane,
Did they
Jump from?
As this
Particular
Group,
Have no
Airplanes,
Or air force,
Is that not
Funny?
Them the creating
Murder and mayhem,
On the innocent
Civilians,
Taking hostages
Back with them,
We pray for
Their safe return,
May they stay
Healthy and
One day again,

Be free!
Now a
Blitzkrieg,
Is underway
Splitting the
World's opinion
Into two camps,
WhileTwo
Thousand pound
Bombs,
Get dropped,
Into a camp,
Packed full,
Of Refugee!
No food,
Water, fuel
Or electricity?
Just Constant
Bombardment,
Ethnic cleansing,
Undoubtedly!
Made up of
Women and
Children mainly!
This has been
Going on
Daily,
For days
Numbering
Thirty!
Death in
One form
Or another?
Seems to be,
An
Inevitability!
Now the
Aicraft carriers
Destroyers,
From many a
"Coalition of
The Willings,"
Navy!
Getting ready

For
World War Three!
Poking the
Bear again,
To a
Greater or
Lesser,
Degree?
The rockets
Will fly!
Where it will end?
Who can see?
While the
West sits at home,
In front of
The TV!
Believing all
On it!
That they
Hear and see!
Getting ready,
For the flu jab
And another one
At the same time,
For the relatively,
Undeadly,
C_V_D!
With a
99 percent
Chance,
If you catch it,
Of Recovery!
Getting us used to
The fifteen minute city!
Low emision zones,
Waiting for cash
To be
Cancelled
The introduction of
CBDC!
Programmable,
Digital
Money,
A Social

Credit Score,
Gone then
Will be,
All
Freedom
And
Liberty!
Weather Warfare,
Now a
Reality!
Extreme Storms,
Droughts,
Floods and
Hurricanes,
As well as
Earthquakes
And Volcanic
Eruptions,
Now a
Commonality!
Plasma,
Created by
Sprayed Metallic
Nano Particulates
In our air,
Then heated up,
By high energy,
Electro Magnetic Frequency!
HAARP,
NEXRAD
and
DOPPLER,
Now positioned
Globally,
Some units
On massive floating
Rig like structures,
With a
Big white dome
On top!
Operating
Invisibly!
GMOs
In our foods,

Sprayed with
Glysophate,
Knowingly!
The introduction of
Crushed insects,
Already,
Reality!
A future where we
Will
"Own
Nothing,
But be,
Happy!
Does that also
Apply to
The
Billionaires
Politician's
And
Royalty?
I doubt that,
So now you see,
Some of,
Our
Enemy!
Our trial
Period in the
New World Order,
Is not
Working out
So greatly!
Check out
Deagal.coms
Future Population
Forecasts
And you
Will see!
A severely,
Diminished
Number of
Living
Human
Beings,
In each

Country!
For the
Perpetrators
Of this
Insanity!
Hell!
Is were you
Will be,
Along with
Your Boss,
For
Eternity!
As the
Gates that are
Pearly!
Will not open
For you,
For destroying,
Others of the
Human race,
Homo Sapiens,
Would you
Not
Agree?

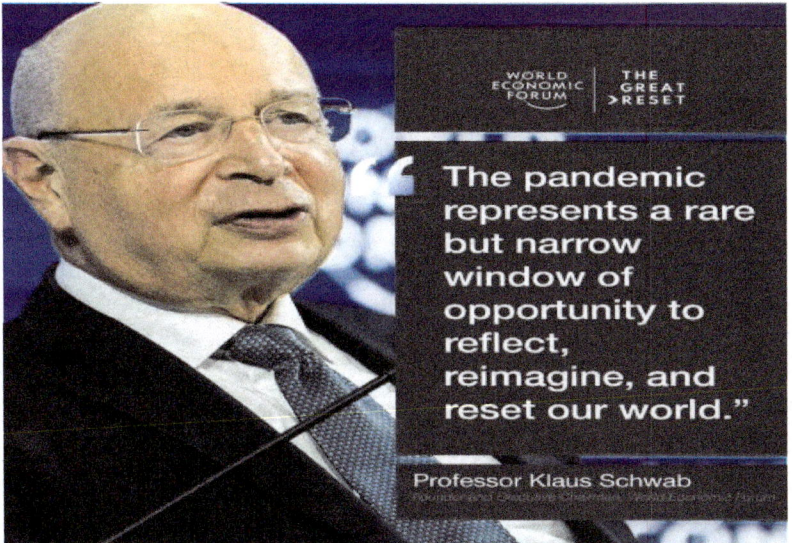

WORLD ECONOMIC FORUM | THE GREAT >RESET

"The pandemic represents a rare but narrow window of opportunity to reflect, reimagine, and reset our world."

Professor Klaus Schwab
Founder and Executive Chairman, World Economic Forum

Air!

We are gathered
Here today
Às Scottish citizens,
Who are trying
To
Awaken
The
Masses,
To the
Ongoing,
Incessant,
Overhead
Spray!
But few
Even take any
Notice of it,
As it is so
Normal now,
Its rarely,
That we see
A clear day!
The
Sun
Being
Hidden
Away!
Geoengineering,
Strategic
Aerosol
Injection
Projects,
Are
Currently,
Underway!
Allowed
By those in
Authority,
Otherwise
The
Spray planes,
Would not

Be able to
Fly so
Freely!
After
Walking
Below
The
Sprays,
We get
Sick
And
Weak!
Including
Our children,
Which on us
People
Of the
Land,
Is not
At all,
Fair!
We
Demand!
That it
Stops!
You
Are

Poisoning,
Our
Air!

All of Humanity!

Robi Smith:
Here's the thing. Nature been doing this pressure and off gassing thing since before mankind was even anything that could affect the process. One single volcano can and has through the natural history of this earth more in hot-house or ice-age ways. The pacific rim f fire has been the largest tecton plate still bobbing around on the subterranean sea of fire for a very very long time.
Sciences theories indicate strongly that as long as tectonic actions are occurring and off gassing off pressure from pumice or clay and rock the less the likelihood of a major eruption. Multiple releases spread out over the earth are better than nothing then suddenly one location/mountain peak let's off too much. Remember not so long ago the Eyjaf_ _ _ _ eruption that shut down the entire northern hemisphere from southern air traffic. That's a very small example of the power of just one volcano.

Hawaii is one of the PRoF major let off points a lot of that action occurs under the ocean. That entire chain of islands earthly activities keep us all between Alaska and Hawaii to California and Vancouver kinda safe. What's going on in the sky doesn't affect what's going on deeper under the earthly mantle. Heck just yesterday Brazil recorded a world record of 58 Celsius I believe. That is all weather tampering whilst volcanic actions have been normal so to speak ...

David:
Thanks for all the information.
We have no control over the Earth's core!
We think that we are the important ones,
You know the score!
Some take the position of God!
Without asking are poisoning
Our global air!
By spraying
Metallic nano particles
And so much more!
Modifying and creating
Weather Warfare!
Using tools like
HAARP, Nexrads,
Doppler's and more!
Many crazy things
We do now see,
From droughts, floods, earthquakes,
Quickly forming hurricanes,
Wildfires and Tsunami!

Playing with natural forces,
Most definitely!
Destroying millions of lives
And home stability!
Leaving millions without a roof
Over their head, globally!
Spraying to block out the Sun,
Which it does most successfully!
Depriving Humanity of their
Ability!
To transfer the
Sunshine
Via the eyes and skin,
Into creating
Vitamin D!
Which our
Immune system needs,
Most definitely!
Underway
Presently,
Is a
Culling of Humanity!
But you shouldn't mess with
Nature as lots will see,
For she will
Recover and
Rebalance,
From any
Catastrophe!
A couple of
Synchronised
Volcanic
Eruptions,
Could be,
Combined
With the
Shite
In our
Skies,
Already,
Become a
Life
Altering
Factor,

For,
All,
Of
Humanity!

All White!

Humza Yusef's speech in the Scottish Parliament!

In it, the SNP MSP complains: "The most senior positions in Scotland in 99 per cent of the meetings I go to, I'm the only non-white person in the room. But why are we so surprised when the most senior positions in Scotland are filled almost exclusively by those who are white?

"Take my portfolio alone. The Lord President - white, the Lord Justice Clark - white, every high court judge - white, the Lord Advocate - white, the Solicitor General - white, the Chief Constable - white, every Deputy Chief Constable - white, every Assistant Chief Constable - white, the head of the Law Society - white, the Head of the Faculty of Advocates -white, every present governor - white. And not just justice.

"The Chief Medical Officer - white, the Chief Nursing Officer - white, the Chief Veterinary Officer - white, the Chief Social Work Advisor - white, almost every trade union in this country headed by people who are white. In the Scottish Government, every director general is white. Every chair of every public body is white. That is not good enough."

Which is why Elon Musk branded him a Racist!

What do you think?

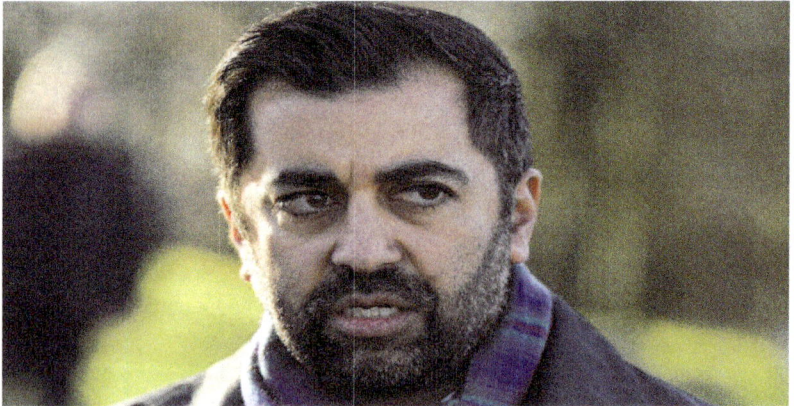

Alright?

"Your weight
Is not bad,
Just have
To lose
Half a
Stone,
To allow
You to
Do the
Free fall,
Skydiving
Flight!"
"Oh
That's
Great,
So I must
Exercise
A bit more!
If I go
Down the
Stairs
For a
Smoke,
Every
Fifteen
Minutes,
Would
That
Be
Alright?"

And Jabs!

THE "I WANT TO DEPOPULATE HUMANITY TO 500 MILLION" STARTER PACK

PROCESSED FOODS

PESTICIDES

FLUORIDE

CHEMTRAILS

@TheTruthWorldOrder

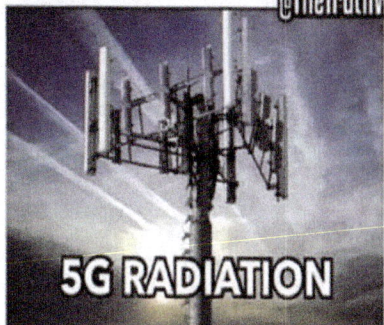

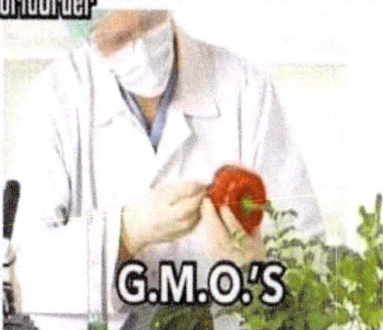

5G RADIATION

G.M.O.'S

And Me!

At one time,
We came
From a
Large family!
With
Uncle's
Aunt's and
Cousin's,
Aplenty!
Headed
At that time,
By
Anne,
My
Granny!
The
MacLeod's,
Nicoll's
And
Long's,
From
66 Seaforth road,
Stornoway,
Are no
Longer,
Living
In the
Plane,
Of the
Earthly!
The
Only
Ones
Left
Now,
Are
Like
The
Last,
Of
The

Mohicans!
Charlie
And
Me!

And See!

Wonder
How long
It will be?
For the
Animal to
Man
Transmission
Claim,
To make
Him a
Zombie?
As a
Thought,
It gives
Plausibility!
For the
Upcoming
Apocalypse,
Let's
Wait
And See!

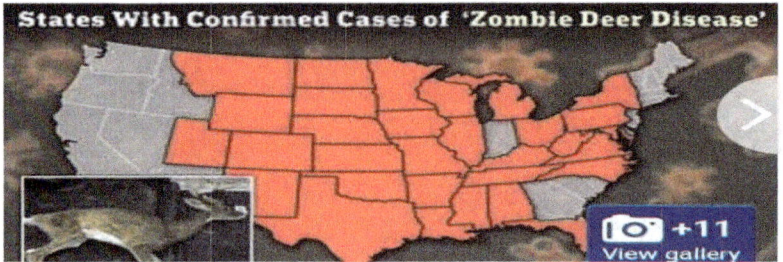

The Deer have all been jabbed! Coincidentally!

Ann's Story!

Ann:
My brother just died suddenly.
Was only 55 He and my other brother looked after my mum so they took all the 💉 😰
He had heart burn one minute then he was gone. I need to say this he looked after my
mum so he took all the 💉 to protect her.

Anymore!

Lost all my
Teeth on top,
My gums
Receded,
You know the
Score!
But,
On the
Bright side,
It cuts
Down on
Dentists
Bill's
And
No
Toothache,
Anymore!

JERRY BREDALE
2001

Appear To Be!

BBC News Report:

Britain has four Vanguard-class submarines – Vanguard, Victorious, Vigilant and Vengeance – with all four based at HMNB Clyde near Helensburgh. One vessel is permanently at sea and all four carry unopened "last instructions" signed by the Prime Minister, giving authorisation to respond with deadly force in the event of a doomsday strike on the UK.

If anyone fires a

Nuclear missile,

At another

Nuclear

Country!

All

Hell will

Break loose,

As from the above

News report,

You can see!

As all the

Nuclear powers,

Will have

Last

Instructions

With

Great

Similarity!

If not

Copying it,

Directly?

So,

It

Only

Takes,

One

Country!

To

Start the

Ping

Pong,

Retribution,

With a

MAD,

Mutually

Assured

Destruction,

Insanity!

With massive

Explosions,

Shock waves,

With

Radiation,

Lasting

Eternally!

Death,

Destruction

An end to

Natural,

Ecology!

That took

Eons

To

Develop,

In

Evolving this

Beautiful

Earths,

Natural

Balance,

What

It was,

In the

Last

Century!

Before

Some of

Mankind,

Got new

Desires,

Like

Power,

Greed,

Control,

Profits

And

Envy!

Many

Royalty

And

Secret

Society!

Satanic

Ritual

Abuse,

And

Adrenochrome

Drinking,

Secretly!

They

Conspired for

World

Control!

Instituting a

"Culling of

Humanity!"

Ongoing

Presently!

Fighting

Wars

By

Proxy!

No bags,

With any

Body,

Coming to

Their shores,

Conveniently,

Laudering

Tax

Payers,

Hard

Earned,

Money!

Making the

Arms

Manufacturers,

Very

Happy!

And the

Many,

Makers of

Pharmacy!

Including

Oor Bill,

Who invested

In them all

Profiting,

Grotesqly!

No doubt,

Making

The

Spirit

Of his

Eugenist

Daddy,

Very

Happy

He started

Planned

Parenthood,

Less people

On the world,

Theywant,

To

See!

Overall

Death

Statistics,

Are rising

Globally!

Jabs and

Boosters,

Needed for

The new,

Digital ID!

Along with a

Digital

Wallet

For your

CBDC*

Your

Vaxxination ID!

Living in a

SMART City,

With

Facial

Recognition,

Being spied on

Constantly,

By all

SMART

Appliences,

Alexa's,

SMART

Meters

And

TV!

Everywhere now

Buzzing with

60 GHz mm,

Microwave

Technology!

Otherwise

Known as

Five

Gee!

Installed

During

Lock Down!

At night,

So that people

Could not see!

But we,

Were

Self imprisoned

In our own

Homes,

Because of an

Invisible

Virus,

Known as

C_V_D!

Very

Conveniently!

The new masts

And lamp posts

Installed at

Warp Speed!

To

Enable,

The

IOT!**

Bringing into it,

The human body!

Via injections,

Containing

Graphene

Oxide,

Which s

Self

Constructs,

Carbon

Nano particle

Tubes,

That we now see,

Taken out by

Morticians on

Cadavers,

Draining

Veins,

In the

Mortuary!

In clear

Glass jars,

Them,

You can see!

No wonder,

So many

Athletes,

Dropped

Dead,

Shaking

Violently!

With it

Happening

To the

Public,

Mainly!

A new

Medical term

Has just

Emerged,

SADS!

Sudden

Adult

Death

Syndrome!

With

Doctors

Baffled,

Conveniently!

Their

Hippocratic

Oath,

Is now

History!

Just waiting for

The

WHO,

To

Declare,

The next

PLANNEDemic,

SCAMMEDemic,

Emergency!

Them

Overriding,

Every nations

Sovereignty!

Declaring

Lock Downs

Anywhere?

Anytime?

That they

Decree!

In

Scotland,

I

Reckon,

They will be,

Beat to it,

By the

SNP!

Scottish

National

Party!

Who retained their

Lock Down Powers

Permenantly!

They will

Utilise that ,

When it

Suits them,

Politically!

In the

Future,

Let's

Just

Wait

And

See!

With

Faslane,

The

Nuclear

Sub port,

Being in

Scotland,

About all the

Above

Listed points,

Do we need to

Worry?

Live for

Today!

Greatfully!

As one day,

It could

Well be?

That

Involved,

In a

MAD

Scenario,

We

Appear,

To Be!

- * Central Bank Digital Currency!
- ** Internet Of Things!

Art by Anon!

Even when you've put your artistic career on hold for a bit, for the sake of your family and kids… it still starts to seep out every way it can… art is just like that 😅

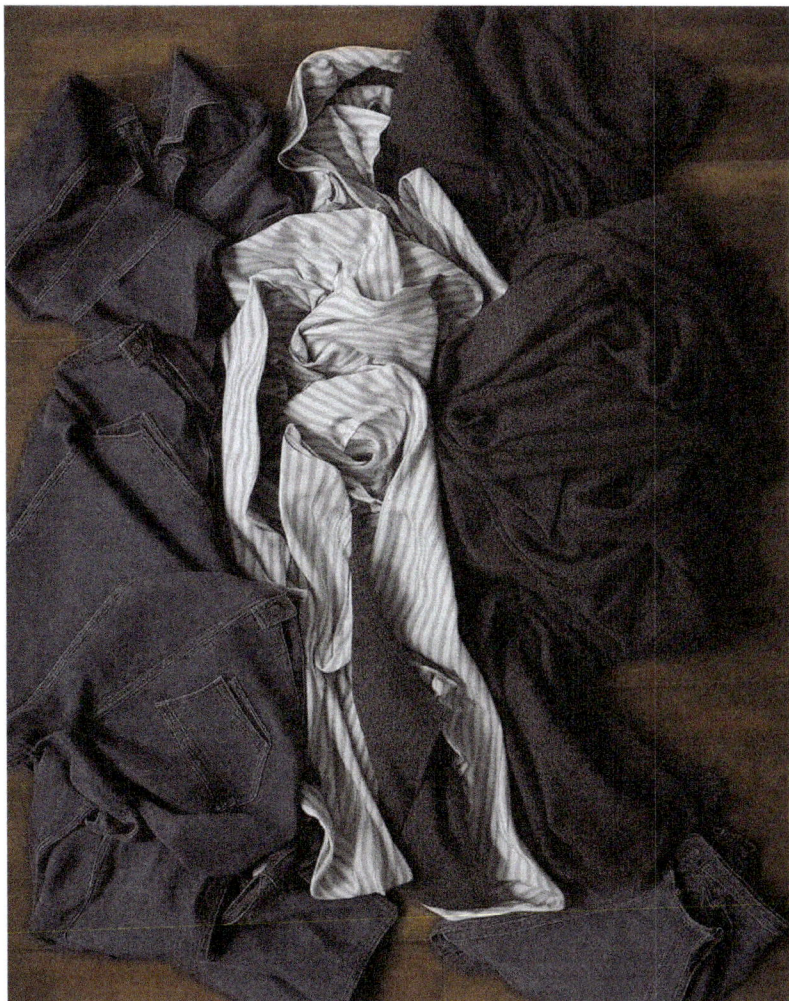

Artificial Snow!

Hilary Peach:
The snow we got up here in the north east of Scotland this last week was in tiny balls like polystyrene, it didn't fall as flakes - it had no crystalline structure, more like softish hailstones.

David:
Three tests to do with it, Try to melt a snowball with a flame, Stick it in a microwave to see if it short circuits and melt it in a clear glass and use a magnet on the outside to attract any metallic nano particles and please video each of the tests.

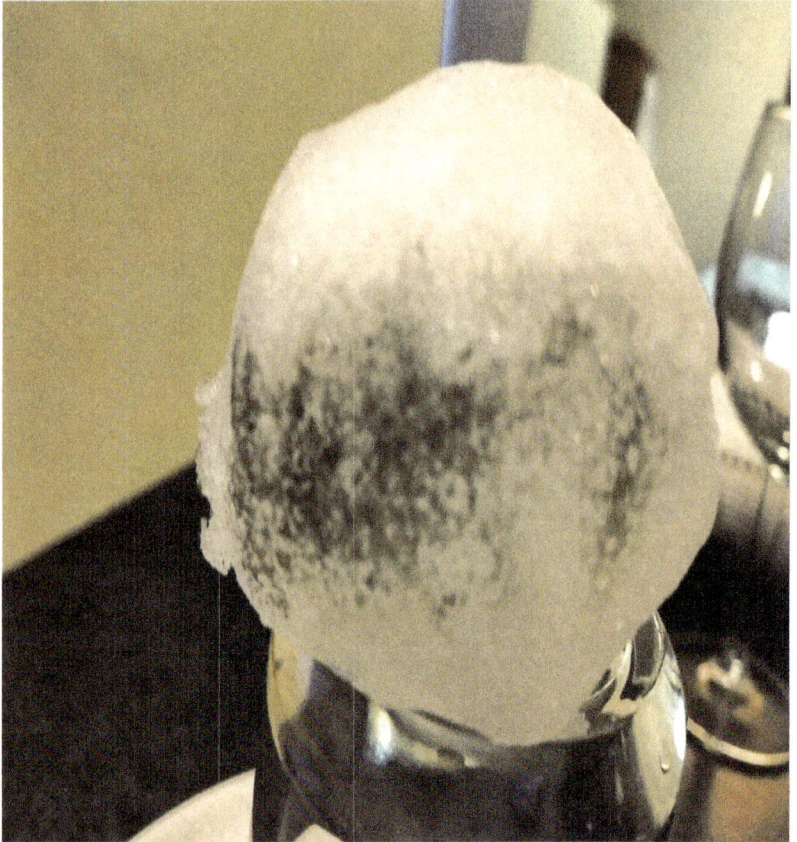

I did a test and ths is what happened to the Snowball!

At Ease!

Just spoke to a
Lady neighbour
In Scotland,
Who used to live
In Madrid,
In
Spain!
She was
Telling me
How the
Heat there,
Used to
Cause
Strain!
"I woke one
Morning at 4am
Couldn't sleep well
The temperature
Was forty one
Degrees!
I looked
Down at
The pool area,
All my
Neighbours
Were in the pool!
Swimming and
Floating,
At
Ease!"

At the End?

Hi Mark, Paul and Lisa I checked out the hotel and it looks fine, three pools, lots of tables with empty glasses for beer, cocktails and wine! Plenty of Sunshine!

A lot ot of people obviously! It's also in a great position to the promenade, beach and harbour. Which we will be frequenting, no doubt daily!

Mark was saying that its all inclusive, flight, accomodation, booze and food! I thought to myself, Oooohhh!!! That sounds good!

Asked him seriously you know, as a Son and friend! "Does it have a bit inside brackets, next to the Signature on the contract that say's,

(Apart from Scotsmen!)

At the End?

Signature .... (Apart from Scotsmen!)

Iberos Las Dalias Hotel. Costa Adaje, Tenerife!

Authority!

They are screwing our children's lives up
In School with teachings of LBGT!
Teaching children about masturbation,
Same sex experimentation and
Anal rimming in Primary!
They are Grooming them, basically!
Nowadays, things are going Crazy!
This just should not be!
I have been to protests
And written about this,
But lots of parents,
Don't even see!
They promote
Sex changes
And can do so,
Without the
Parents
Know how,
Or
Authority?
In Scotland,
You can get your
Sex change
Operation,
For Free!
Paid for
By the SNP!
Getting them
Ready,
For the
Paedophiles,
That are in
Authority!

Awry!

Coming soon, but no one knows when? The cancellation of Pounds, Dollars and Yen! To a cashless society, to be controlled, Digitally! Utilising CBDC!* Programmable to control you, completely! Living in SMART City, a part of the IOT!** Not being implemented lovingly, Obviously! But a big part of Agenda 2021 and 30! Where the WEF can fulfill their plan of us "Owning Nothing, but being Happy!" The WHO ready, to declare a PLANNEDemic Emergency, Anywhere, Anytime? With no thought for National Sovereignty! Declaring Lock Down terms and Injections that would be, Mandatory! Making the makers and shareholders of Pharmacy, very rich and Happy! Going from one, to another war, by Proxy! Selective Genocide underway, presently! With the Wests approval and backing, apparently!

Illegal immigrants, flooding many a land and city! Creating No Go zones, in Sweden currently! With the Rape Capital of Europe being a title, that it holds, currently! Them being given in the UK, Four star hotel accommodation, for free! Spending money, freedom to do as they wish, while waiting on Asylum approval, by those, in Authority! Some say, by stealth, a UN Army? Creating problems, already, with many, a local community! Our bloodstock being diluted, Undoubtedly!

The sudden introduction of 60GHz mm Microwave Technology! Otherwise known as Five Gee! Installed hastily, by men in white vans, during Lock down, at night, so no one could see! Masts appearing suddenly! Installed at Warp speed, globally!

While our skies get sprayed, daily! Invisibly to the majority, who have eyes, that cannot see! Programmed, Brainwashed, Hypnotised and Bamboozled by their ever present and always on, Telly! Believing all on it, that they hear and see! "They are CONtrails only!" They all agree! Part of the ongoing Culling of Humanity! Underway, presently! With global overall death rates, rising Exponentially! Our air being Poisoned by soft metal nano particulates, breathed in easily! While the so called Vaxxinations against C_V_D, putting millions, Prematurely, into the Crematorium or Cemetery? While millions of other, lives now ruined, Permanently! Where, pre jab, they were Healthy! When asking, "Could this be, to do with the jab?" They are told, "That cannot, possibly be!" Big moves underway currently! Controlled by an evil entity! But Fortunately there are those, with open eyes, that can see! Whose bloodstreams are still the way, that they should be! Watching the moves, like a playbook, bringing us into World War Three! To control the masses, divide and rule, philosophy! A new King for the world, soon we shall see! A one world religion, Chrislam, coming shortly! A narrow window of opportunity said Klaus and Charlie! With a distinct Possibility that the best laid plans of mice and men said by Rabbie, "Aft Gang Awry!"

*=Central Bank Digital Currency!

**=Internet Of Things!

Scottish Scaffolder Alex Mitchell, Vaxxine injured!

Be!

I was wanting
To visit
An old lady,
Who was a friend
Of my parents,
In my
Family!
"Do you have all
The protections
In place for
C_V_D?"
She wanted
To see!
"Do you mean
Vaxxinations?"
"Yes!"
She replied,
"No!"
Was said
By me!
"We could
Always wear
Masks!"
"I don't
Do that
Either,
Unfortunately!"
So Alas,
Our planned
Meeting,
Is not,
Going
To
Be!

Be Empty!

Scotlyn O'Daniel:
Yeah, that was when the hospitals were

"Overflowing with patients".

So much so they had time to practice their dance moves.

David:

The hospital's

Were full,

Supposedly,

Until some

Activist's

Went in with

Videos and

Found them

To be,

Empty!

Beat!

"Fag,
Piss,
Drink,
Then
Repeat!"
Old
Age,
Can't
Be
Beat!

Before!

Fiona Buzza:
David Nicoll yes indeed, as I've just received it today Tuesday 9th January!! Wishing everybody on this site a very Happy New Year xx

Pauline Rodger Davis:
Just got a notification about this 2 hours ago..hope all was well with yours David.

David:
Maybe
Next year,
Now that
We know the
Score!
I will send out
Our SMAAPP
Happy Christmas
Greetings,
Two weeks
Before!

Between!

Being a
Digital
Nomad,
Is
Not,
So
Bad!
Three
Months
In
Scotland,
Then
Three
In
Tenerife,
Never
Sad!

Loving
Life,
Here
And
There,
A
Great
Scene!
On
Holiday
Permanently!
But
With
Work
Breaks,
In
Between!

Bio for Jesse Hal of The Missing Link!

David was born in Stornoway, the Isle of Lewis, Scotland in February 1954.
Then moving to Edinburgh for his teenage years and serving his apprenticeship as an
Architectural technician with the two main restoration and conservation architects in
Scotland.
After a prompt from a friend he then moved over to piping design and after a
discussion with a
Depressed man in the refinery in Grangemouth he was inspired to move to South
Africa.
Newly married and with a young son, he then left Scotland in February 1982 looking for
greener pastures, sunshine and adventure.
After living and working in Johannesburg for many years, including working in Kenya
and Tanzania, he became disillusioned with the rat race and left to move to
KwaZuluNatal.
After attending TJs folk club in Johannesburg he formed the band Hakuna Matata with
three great guitarists and singers. They played at various festivals including Splashy fen
and Womad in Benoni and recorded a CD titled Ecology.
Poetry for him came as a surprise and was initially discovered when writing to clear out
his mind, it came out as Poetry. He was then introduced to playing the African Djembe
drum, which resonates with his Soul. These gifts were then combined to do both at the
same time.
On arriving in Newcastle, KZN, he noticed that there was no live music anywhere there,
so he started the Newcastle Folk n Culture club with new friends and workmates. This

culminated in a band known as US (United Souls) performing initially at the Southern Cross music festival and then at Splashy fen, Rustlers valley and Flux festivals. The number of performers in the band varied greatly with many very talented musical friends joining us on stage. A lot of the highly talented drummers from the Durban Drumshack also contributed to the highly charged performances. Recordings were made of some of their live events.

He loves designing and building, while in Johannesburg along with a new son and daughter, bought an old property with hardwood floors, refurbished it, renamed it as The Croft and built a large vegetable garden to supply food for his family as well as hens to supply eggs. This property had a swimming pool, which was in fact the trigger for moving there after getting told by the depressed man in Grangemouth that some people had them in their back gardens. He was depressed because he had been there and was now living in a third floor flat in Falkirk and catching the bus to work.

His wife became disillusioned with life in South Africa and homesick so she returned to her birthplace with his children in 1994.

Years later he bought the topside of a hill just inland from Durban in the valley of a thousand hills and after moving in a back acter JCB, proceeded to create platforms using the cut and fill method, while shaping the ground to collect all the storm water. Along with a good friend Keith Roderick, a great djembe drummer and landscaper they built an eco house with living walls utilising all the local materials and building a Black house using the dug out rock and earth infill as the walls. The structures were designed to minimise on wind shear and the land was used for food production including a highly stocked orchard. While there he bought a female pure white Artic Wolf female puppy and then later got a pure black Canadian TimberWolf male pup. They then bred and he kept some of the beautiful hybrid pups. This property was called The Irie Eyrie! It had an amazing 300 degree view over the valleys.

Then moving to Mossel bay in the garden route, he worked in the refinery there and had the pleasure of visiting and enjoying beautiful places like Knysna, Plettenberg bay and Wilderness.

On one trip to Knysna he noticed some long white streaks in the sky and wondered what they were? After asking a lady who was posting photos of these, she suggested that he looked up Geoengineering. This suggestion turned out to be a real eye opener for him.

After getting laid off from his job in 2017 and waiting for a year to find work in a depressed economy, he was faced with the realisation that returning to Scotland was the only option.

When returning to Scotland and living in his oldest sons flat, he noticed the absolute carnage that was happening in the Glasgow skies. They were criss crossed daily by long white spreading streaks in the sky which would form a chemical silver grey haze and block out the Sun. The craziest thing was that hardly anyone noticed them or even mentioned them. After meeting some new freinds from Anti Geoengineering Scotland it was decided to form a Facebook group called SMAAPP Scottish Musicians and Artistes Against the Poisoning of our Planet. We then started our SMAAPP Live Awareness gigs, the first being in the Clutha bar in Glasgow in November 2018 to raise awareness about the Geoengineering insanity. SMAAPP has now grown to over 3,500 global members who are aware and awake to a lot of the issues that we face today. There are great posts about the these issues as well as performance music videos. If you have an open mind, you are welcome to join us.

He has worked in Norway and Germany and noticed that they also get heavily sprayed with the same disinterest from the public, who seem to not notice the sprays at all and when you mention it to them, they say that they are contrails. His feeling is that this is indoctrination by the TV! He has not watched TV since 1982.

Several more SMAAPP events were held with great performances by local Poets and Musicians.

These then morphed into Create for Truth events, held at the Avant Garde restaurant in Glasgow.

They were attended by many from the Freedom movement in Scotland. Initially the meetings were against Lock down as that was the pertinent issue at that time. We had many great evenings with brilliant performances and it gave us a chance to socialise with people of a like mind.

Upon getting laid off at the start of Lock down, he decided to become a full time poet, writing about all the current issues from a truthful perspective. He likes to say that he was producing books the same way as a hen lays eggs, on a very regular basis and has gone on to produce a large number of Scottish Thoughts and Reflection books, POKEs POetic joKE books as well as Geoengineering Poetry and Photos Vols 1 and 2. These have been used as conversation starters by others to try to awaken their friends.

His oldest son set up a website for him and all of his creations can be found there in books and CDs, it is www.davidnicoll.co.uk

While in South Africa he created the CDs David Nicoll and friends Vols 1, 2 and 3 with many great friends and musicians as well as six CDs with a retired singer songwriter called Mervyn Fuller in a collaboration known as MAD Mervyn And Dave, they are listed as Mervyn Fuller and David Nicoll, where he was the lyricist and would write the lyrics after prompts from Mervyn, who would then produce the songs, they are all available on Spotify.

He is currently on a working holiday in Tenerife and has noted that they also get sprayed there.

YouTube were so impressed with some of his online book launches that they closed his channel completely two years ago. They don't like the Truth getting out and he likes to weave it into the

Word Tapestry in his Poetry.

THE MISSING
LINK

Host

JESSE
HAL

David Nicoll

Thoughts
and
Reflections

ol 2

avid Nicoll

Thursday November
30th @ 1pm EST

Birthday!

Off to Stornoway
Next week for about
A ten day stay!
To celebrate with
My children and
Grandchildren,
My
Three
Score
Years,
Plus
Ten,
Birthday!

Bloody!

Julie Cox:
Except its not nature. Now these people are supposed to be clever and educated with
degrees. So I have to ask the question, are they in the know and normalising this crap,
or are they not that really educated and not that clever?

David:
They don't know about Geoengineering and Weather Warfare. At there cellphone
screens, they blankly stare! They believe all that they hear and see, on their own TV!
"It's only CONtrails!" They all Agree! Thanking God, for the unreal sights, symbols,
shapes and colours in our skies, that we now see! Following the narrative, daily! First it
was Lock Downs, Wear masks and stay six feet, away from me! Don't visit your family,
not even Granny! Take an unauthorised, So called vaxxine against C_V_D! It started
with one, but now it is many! Take Furlough money! Ignore the suicides and mass
middle man's business bankruptcy! The vaxxine injured being ignored and left to
suffer, in Solitary! While many thousands of others, now either in a Crematorium or
Cemetery? Increasing Overall death counts now a global, Commonality! The doctors
are all Baffled, apparently! While pocketing, quietly, for giving the jabs, loads of
Money! They and the nurses giving them, involved in crimes against Humanity! All
done, in the name of OUR Health and Safety! The government's and MSM also
involved implicitly! The WHO, WEF and UN following a New World Order, Philosopy!
The ongoing implementation, of Agenda 2021 and 30! To tie us all down, in a SMART
fifteen minute, CITY! Where we, will "Own nothing, but be, Happy !" With no cash
anymore, only CBDC!* With a Social Credit Score, as it is in China, currently! All

SMART devices, listening and watching you, Constantly! Zero Privacy! Everywhere buzzing with a targeted weapons system, known as Five Gee! Masts installed, surreptitiously, during Lock down, at night, so that people, would not see! The 60GHz mm Microwave Technology, capable of varying frequency! Affecting the Graphene Oxide in the jabs, now in Billions of people's veins, where it should not be! Also capable of affecting the metallic nano particulates sprayed via Geoengineering, into our global skies, daily, Inhaled, easily, then absorbed into the bloodstream and body! The Elderly and disabled, Euthenased, illegally! Using Midazolam and Morphine cocktails, administered, eagerly! To enhance the death charts and ramp up the fear, in those watching the Telly! Pot and pan banging, on Thursday evenings, becoming socially, Mandatory! While the hospital staff get choreographed dance lessons and make Tik Tok videos, during a PLANNEDemic, SCAMMEDemic, Emergency! Look at the 2012 London big show at Wembley! They could not have told us, more plainly! Hundreds of hospital beds, a massive devil with wand and what we now know as a close up, of the as then unknown atom, of C_V_D! Giving us clues, cryptically! Then all of a sudden, no more of it, do we see! Because of the world's population, they had injected, in percentage terms, six plus sixty! Then all the worlds focus of attention was changed to a war, fought by Proxy! Funnelling hundreds of Billions of dollars in Armaments for their military! Making the Arms manufacturer's very, happy! They want War, constantly! The Political Puppets getting kickbacks, in the form of money! Laundering tax payers, money! Making them Millionaires, very quickly! Where they got the cash from? They cannot answer, easily! At that time, there was a possibility Of World War Three? If someone should fire a Nuclear warhead, deliberately or accidentally? Now the war in the Northern hemisphere is on the back burner, against what in the Middle East, we now see! The most heavily armed state, getting attacked by its prisoner's in a concentration camp, down by the Mediterranean sea! Border crossing left open and empty! Very strangely! As the country is invaded by many, Armed men, driving a lot of white brand new looking, white SUV! Has anyone asked where they got them from? There are no new car dealerships inside there, you see! Or how paratroopers, rained down, Supposedly, from a terrorist group with no air force or planes, to aid its army? Questions worth asking, would you not agree? They shot and killed many, took lots of hostages, an atrocity! Could it be, possibly? That this was done, by prearrangement, coordination and planning, previously! To enable a further, much larger, atrocity! Using right of defence to slaughter thousands if not millions ultimately? To make land grabs, illegally! To mow down, the population, with constant bombing, starvation, dehydration, disease and dysentry? To flatten the buildings, Completely? This is still underway, Currently! With no food, water, fuel or electricity! The innocent civilian men, women and children, die needlessly! Not even aware, of the recent atrocity! The western world getting ready, for an Escalation of combat, for which they are getting ready! By moving aircraft carrier's and gunships into the East Mediterranean Sea! All behind the two triangle flag, Obviously! Make war by deceit! Is indeed the way, that it seems to be! Like the war on terror, started after nine eleven, where TWO planes brought down massive steel and concrete skyscrapers, numbering THREE! Does no-one find that odd, or funny? How the world can be fooled, so easily! The outcome of this, is not clear to see, other than a knowing, that it will be, bloody!

*= Central Bank Digital Currency

Bonus!

Nicola had a
Fifty Euro note
Tucked in
Her shoe!
'Why don't you
Put it in your
Nickers?
That you
Could do!"
'It would be
Less
Crumpled,
With a lot
Less fuss!
And for any
Potential,
Partner's,
Fifty
Euros
In her
Nickers,
Would
Be
A
Real,
Bonus!

Book Review of Tenerife Thought's and Reflections Vol 2 Part 1 by Greg Toombs!

5.0 out of 5 stars Book review of Tenerife Thought's and Reflections Vol 2 Part 1

Reviewed in the United States on February 14, 2024

I have followed David for a few years now as he writes about his adventures and his perception of these experiences. I am able to see what he is speaking about vividly, so well in fact; it is almost like being there. The things David writes about; are in synch with everything I see on this other half of the world as well; issues are GLOBAL. This world will become a better place when his educational poetry books are seen in school libraries. People should NEVER be targeted for speaking the truth. This book of poetry is another masterpiece in a large group of other poetry books he has written. Each and every book has meaning and a purpose. I enjoyed the book David, another job WELL DONE! I recommend this book to almost everyone, from a novice up to other poets and literary folk. ENJOY!!! By Greg Toombs.

Tenerife Thoughts and Reflections Vol 2 Part 1 Hard Cover

David Nicoll

David has had numerous poems
published in South African and
International publications and was
included in the International
Who's Who of Poetry in 2012

This is the Second in a series of Tenerife
Thoughts And Reflections books. This
book contains Thought Provoking
Poetry some with Photographs.
Subjects Including Geoengineering,
Current and Global Affairs, Adventures,
Tourist pursuits, friends,
performers and some POKEs POetic
joKEs to give You a laugh! For the rest of
his Books, CDs, Performance Videos,
Online Book Launches, Lyric videos,
Book Reviewers And Body Art/Tattoos
section, Please visit his
website:www.davidmcoll.co.uk or see

ISBN 9798875951640

90000

9 798875 951640

Brick!

You know,
In life
Its not cool
To be thick!
The powers
That be,
When they see
This book,
Vol 20!
Are
Going
To
Shit,
A
Brick!

Brilliant!

Said by a tourist
From California,
Who in the toilet
At Oran mor
With his mate
Was having a
Blether!
"Everything
About
Scotland is
Brilliant,
Apart
From the
Weather!"
Then,
Without
A
Pant,
"The
People

In
Scotland,
Are
Brilliant!"

By Me!

Ref: DPD9704431

Good Morning,

I hope you're doing well.

Our depot advised that unfortunately the shipment has been declared as lost. To proceed, we will file a claim for this. Could you please provide the following details below:

Please provide a full description of the contents. including the number of items in the parcel, colour, size, make, model numbers, media titles, and any other distinguishing features.

-Provide a full description of the packaging. This should include details such as material (cardboard box, jiffy bag, other), packaging colour, tape colour, additional labels or writing on the packaging.

-Parcel Value

Apologies for this inconvenience. Looking forward to hearing from you.

Kindest Regards Jaysa

Hi Jaysa

I am extremely disappointed and frustrated at your

Not being able to do what you were contracted to do.

Which is to deliver my parcel to Jesse Hal in Calgary!

For me giving you an incorrect email contact details initially,

I apologize profusely!

But you were given his correct details

Including phone number

When requested of me!

But you never contacted him!

Why?

Is a Mystery?

It did have the correct

Address on it though!

But did you EVER Actually,

Try to deliver it?

You did not

Apparently!

In the Royal mail system,

The address,

Is all that is necessary!

The contents are

Four published books of my

Original Poetry!

Priced at fifteen pounds each,

Plus the cost of me

Sending it,

Which in pounds

Is Eighty!

Needless to say,

Your services,

Will

NEVER

AGAIN,

Be used

By me!

4x15=60 plus 80 = 140 British Pounds refund!

By Money!

The
Doctors
Are always
Baffled,
Which is
Funny!
Silenced,
By
Money!

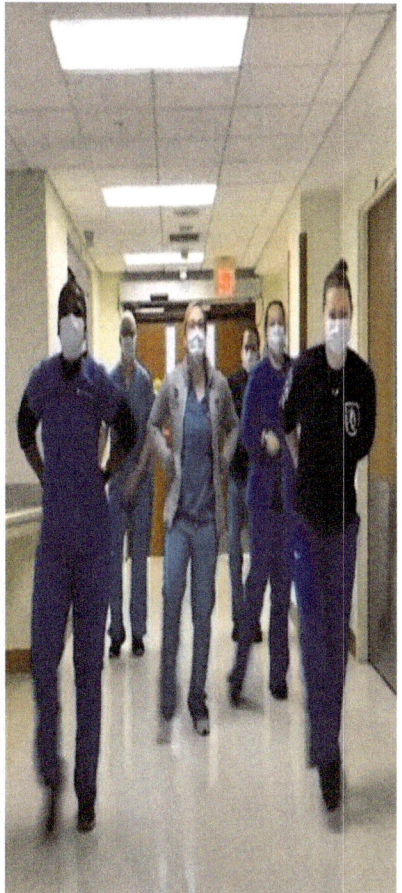

Casualty!

To be or
Not to be?
Between
The so called
Vaxxinated and
Unvaxxinated!
There is a

Chasm,
That we,
Can now
See!
A programme
Against the
Latter,
Was
Implemented,
Politically!
With all the
WEF,
WHO,
And
UN!
Pulling
The
Politician's
Strings,
As in
Puppetry!
All shouting
The same,
Decree!
The
Truth,
Being
Inverted,
Obviously!
Saying that
The
Former,
Were in
Danger,
From the
Latter,
Is a
Lie!
That
Now,
We
Can
See!
Because

"Shedding!"
Is now
Reality!
So it is
The other
Way round,
Precisly!
The only
Ones that
Now catch
C_V_D!
Have been
Vaxxinated
Against it,
Is that
Not
Funny?
People now
With
SADS*
Where did
That come from?
Them
Dropping dead,
Shaking
Violently!
Athletes and
Sportsmen
We do
See!
Headed
To the
Crematorium or
Cemetry?
People
In the
Prime
Of their
Lives,
Healthy,
Previously!
Millions
Of others
Globally!

Are no longer
On this
Earth
But in it!
As from the
Increasing
Overall
Death
Statistics,
We can see!
But the
Owners
Of
Pharmacy,
Including
Oor Bill,
Are
Greedy!
During the
Last
PLANNEDemic,
SCAMMEDemic,
Emergency!
After issuing
The MRNA,
DNA
Altering,
Witches
Concoctions,
Their
Profits rose,
Stratospherically!
Remember the
Georgia
Guidestones,
Future
Population
Forecasts,
That
"They"
Would like
To see!
A
Ninety five

Percent
Reduction,
In
Gobal
Humanity,
By the year
2030!
They
Demolished them
Quite
Conveniently!
By a
Miracle?
Apparently!
Or a
DEW?
As used in
Paradise,
California,
And
Maaui,
Recently!
Which melts
Windshield glass
And
Aluminium
Wheel hubs,
Easily!
Silent
Weapons,
For
Quite
Wars!
Philosopy!
While our
Water is
Flouridated
And
Skies
Sprayed,
Daily!
With
Metallic
Nano

Particles,
Inhaled
Easily!
Creating a
Coagulation of
Aluminium
In the
Brain!
Dementia and
Althzheimers
Numbers,
Rising
Exponentially!
Does anyone
Ever ask,
"How did it
Get there?"
Where it,
Should
Not be?
The
Doctors
Are
Baffled!
We hear
Frequently!
Them
Taking the
Money!
Dance lessons
For
Nurses and
Doctors,
Apparently,
Were
For
Free!
This
During an
Emergency!
Where the
Hospitals
Were
Full up!

Supposedly,
But lots
Found
To be,
Empty!
The 2012
Olympic
Opening,
Ceremony,
In
London,
Gave us
Big clues,
Of what
Was
To be!
Look at it
Again,
In
Retrospect
And you
Will see!
Prewarning us,
Of what
Was
To be!
Event 201
A
Precursor,
Coincidentally,
To the
PLANNEDemic
Emergency!
Run by
Bill and
Klaus,
His big
Buddy!
God had
To move over,
When Bill,
Used to
Come on
TV!

Telling the
Whole of
Humanity!
"No one is
Safe until
Everyone
Has been
Jabbed!"
He did
Decree!
Like a
Vaxxine
Salesman,
Which
He is,
Apparently,
Investing
In the
Seven main,
Vaxxine
Manufacturers,
Then
Profiting,
Stratospherically!
Killing two
Birds with
One stone,
Mentality!
Now
Klaus,
Apparently
Seems,
To be,
Thinking that
He is
Something,
That we,
Should
Envy!
Boasting of
His
Infiltrating
Cabinets,
In many

A country!
This,
We can now,
Hear and see!
By their
Agreement,
On
Policy!
No
Opposition
To talk of,
Where now
Is
Democracy?
We have
Been told,
That we,
Will
"Own
Nothing,
But be
Happy!"
Eat
Crushed
Insects,
Ground
Crickets,
In the
Goods,
On
Supermarket
Shelves,
Already!
Read your
Ingredients,
Carefully!
Also from
The WEF and
UN!
Agenda 2021
And 30!
Where we,
Will live,
In a

SMART,
City!
Well
Underway,
Already!
Human
Rights
And
Freedoms,
Being
Eroded
Daily!
Children
Getting
Groomed
In school,
Taught a
Curriculum of
LBGT!
Promoting
Sex change
Operations,
Which
Create,
Sterility!
Perverting
Their minds,
For
Ulterior
Motives,
Like for
Paedophilles,
In
Authority!
My how
The
World
Has
Been
Changed,
Since
March
2020!
Where we

Were
Lied to
By
Boris,
Profusely!
"Lets shut
Down for
Weeks,
Numbering
Three!
To
Flatten
The
Curve!"
Our
Imposed
Self imprisonment
With
Ever changing
Rules,
Regulations
And
Fines!
Changing
Frequently!
Priming us,
For the
"Fifteen
Minute
City!"
Suicides,
Unemployment,
Bankruptcy!
Big
Brother
Is now
Running
The
Show!
As
George
Orwell
In his
Book

1984
Did
Forsee!
We have
The
War by
Proxy!
The five
Minutes
Of hate
Figure
Being
Vladimir P,
Temporarily!
The
Tele screens,
Give instructions
And spy
On you,
Constantly!
Along with all
Your
SMART
Appliences,
Secretly!
A
New
World
Order
And
NATO
Its
Army!
Now
Sretching
Its
Tentacles,
To parts
Of the
World,
Where it,
Should
Not be!
Needing

Supplies of
Natural gas,
With a
Planned
Pipeline,
Under
The
Mediterranean
Sea,
Landing in
Italy!
From as yet
Untapped,
Enormous
Reserves,
Owned
Offshore
In
Gazza,
By the
Displaced
Palestinians,
Now
Living as a
Community,
With the
Status
Of
Refugee!
The
MSM
And
Media,
Controlled
Totally,
Misleading
The
Masses,
The
Majority,
Giving them
Eyes,
That
Cannot

See!
Programmed,
Brainwashed,
Hypnotised and
Bamboozled,
By their
Own
Telly!
Where
Right
Is
Wrong,
Black
Is
White,
And
Truth,
Is
The
Casualty!

*= Sudden Adult
Death Syndrome!

Cemetery!

Just learned
Something
Yesterday,
That before,
I did not know!
The one place,
That you
Don't want
Your name
Appearing,
Too soon,
Is in this
Central
Stornoway,
Butcher's
Window!
It tells
Of where
The services
Will be held,
Once you
Are
Deceased,
No more
To see
And at
What
Cemetery?

BLYTHSWOOD
SERVICE 11am
DONALD A. MACMILLAN
MARTIN'S MEMORIAL CHURCH
SERVICE 2pm
MARGARET M. MACKAY
SERVICE 11.30am
MALCOLM M. SMITH
BARVAS
CHURCH OF SCOTLAND
SERVICE 11.30am
FRIDAY 9th FEBRUARY
Fridays at the Free
MA HALL
12-3pm
Free soup/roll, tea, coffee
& Baby Bank items
Newspapers, books, free WIFI
Board games, play area for
children of all ages.
ALL WELCOME

Cheaply!

Sending my love, you all I look forward to see! Next February! When my age on the earth will be, Seventy! Blessed to here, still be, alive and healthy! We could have a Party! Looking forward to next April as well, when this beautiful place, you will all see! Going to. hire a yacht, for us all, to go out to Sea! It is great to see the Dolphins and Whales, swimming free! then swimming and snorkeling in a beautiful bay. when Patrick. the skipper, puts out Beer, wine, snacks, on the way back the beautiful massive Volcano of Tiede! You will love it here! that is why the place I would like you to all see! A break in the Sunshine,
Pretty
Cheaply!

Cheer!

"I am going out
Tonight to celebrate
A friend's birthday!"
Is what my daughter
Lisa had to say!
Later that night
I poked my head
Into the Crit bar,
Then left but
Didn't get far!
"Dad,
Dad,
I am
Here!"
Which
Certainly
Left us
Both,
In
Good,
Cheer!

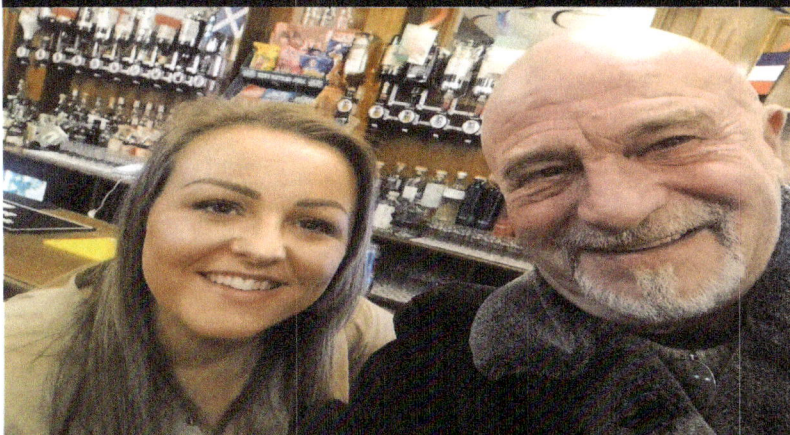

David Nicoll
Had the pleasure of meeting with my daughter
Lisa last night.

148   16 comments

❤️ Love   💬 Comment   ⊘ Send   ↗ Share

Christmas Presents!

Sherron Wallace Southwark:

I took 3 of your books Christmas & read some of your work to my daughter & son-in-law.

I tried to show the titles but failed.

David:

Oh that is so lovely Sherron, thank you so much and I am honoured that you want to educate the youngsters. I am so interested to see what ones that you chose? Please take a photo of them and another couple of you with them.

Library!

David:
Great photo of you Sherron Wallace Southworth did Father Christmas bring you the book?

Sherron Wallace Southwark:
David, Thank you & yes, he did indeed. Fancy that! Scottish Thoughts & Reflections Vol 1- Rev 1, Vol 2 & 5. (Others are near the gifts.) As my precious daughter, ByJennifer Lynn prepared Christmas dinner, I opened the 1st in the middle with "Barium and Strontium", & "Irretrievably!" Now that I look back so fitting as are all. Thank you for bringing to light the plight within plain sight through your poems & songs. (I've never written a poem in my life but there's a bit.)

David:
Sherron Wallace Southworth careful if you read, too much, Poetry, it could be, Contagious? As it, with you, appears to be! These books contain, History! Of the time, when they were written, telling of the Lock Down times, restrictions on our Freedom and Liberty! Thank you Sherron for buying them and adding, to your, Library!

Any reviews
Would be
Appreciated,
Most

Gratefully!

Sherron reading Scottish Thoughts and Reflections Vol 1

Scottish Thoughts and Reflections Vol 1 Rev 1

Black and white photos

David Nicoll

The cover photo is a Geoengineered sky over Glencoe in Scotland.

Co-incidence?

Jay Deen:

An interesting

Anagram for

Chemtrails is..

Metals Rich.

Co-incidence ?

Coke!

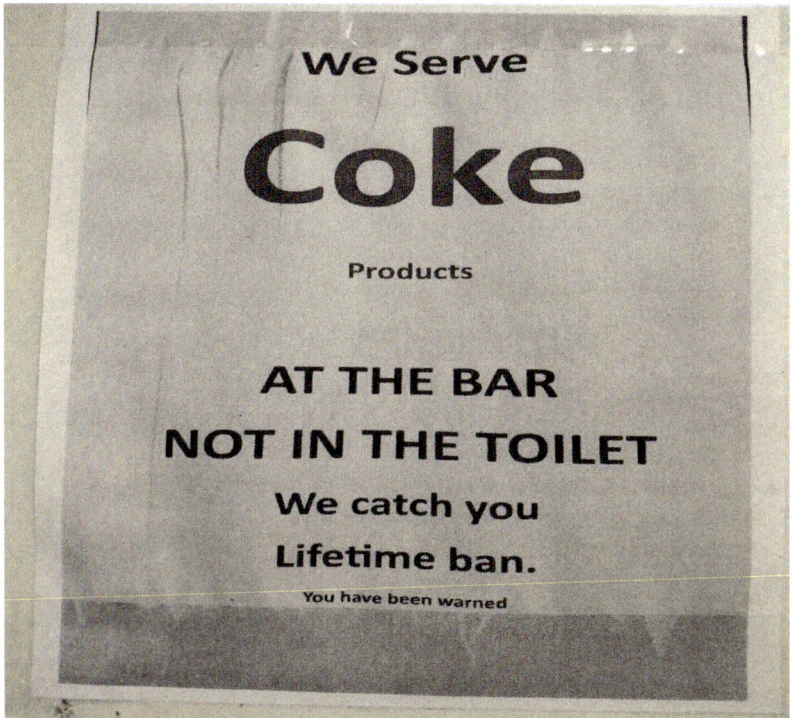

We Serve
Coke
Products

**AT THE BAR
NOT IN THE TOILET**
We catch you
Lifetime ban.
You have been warned

Comment by Minx Millar:

Thank you David for the amount of time that you spend making people aware of the truth - you do it in such a loving way and i do respect and admire you for that - May you be blessed with love courage and strength to continue with your work as an earth angel on the planet - may the people just start asking questions - and may we be saved from this man made insanity - lots of love to you David x x x x x

Comments on my Amazon Author page!

Scotland O'Daniel:
Wow! Quite a few out there. Nice! I will try to get that review done after the holidays, but great job David! Amazing work and pieces of recorded history.

Sherron Wallace Southwark:
Thank you for the books!

Comments on Appearing on The Missing Link!

Laura Huber-Kimball:
I'm looking forward to your interview! This is SO awesome, David!!
TY for the advance notice.
So looking forward to it!

Janine Andrews:
You legend! Keep shining that brilliant light David!

Alan Serge McGhee:
Get in there David!

Scotlyn O'Daniel:
Congrats! Can't wait to watch it. It's going to be good!

Miriam Erasmus:
Perfect!

Momo Clark:
Looking forward to this David.
Can't wait lol, you're famous!

Mark Whitby:
Nice one brother.

Comments on my Poetry!

Scotlyn O'Daniel:
You are on a roll with them and that is wonderful!
All of your books are a piece of history that they
Can't erase so easily. So screw them.

Laura Huber-Kimball:
Such wisdom must come from those who've experienced it and when we share this
knowledge it goes into the hearts of others to go out and achieve THEIR dreams! Good
on you, David!

Comments on the poem titled Constantly!

Tiffany Shepard:
Brilliant poem David.

Chris Prior:
Good one, lad.

Laura Huber-Kimball:
Seeing this video today I NOW understand your poem's reference to using bombs to
create a new shipping canal in or next to Gaza; I did NOT know this reference when I
first read "Constantly." Very spot-on writing, David. Man's greed has no bounds.

Comments on the poem titled Necessary!

David Yates:
Yet another epic Dave.

David:
Thank
You!
Sad
But

True!

Miriam Erasmus:
Spot on as usual.

Asia S Boni:
When you write, it always resonates. Keep it up please, David.

Sonya Davalos:
I'm so proud of you David Nicoll xx

Comments on the poem titled To See!

Leanne Costa:
Beautifully put, David.

Laura Huber- Kimball:
I wish I could support David's work financially however I'm VERY pleased to be able to do so with my voice! David's poetry is whimsical, heartwarming, honest, telling and entertaining! Depending which poem we read we can feel the whole range of human emotions and we can relate to his words, I've enjoyed several of his writings throughout many shares on social media and I can honestly say I have NEVER been disappointed in his words. I highly recommend you seek out his works, buy some if you're able to both support him and to have a written record of what the powers that be have been and are currently doing to humanity in case they scrub these truths from the internet. Having books to show posterity will help ensure new generations won't be denied this knowledge.

Commodity!

Lia Farrel:
Fair play to you getting
Published.

David:
I became a full time poet on the 23rd of March 2020, the day that Lock Down started, to keep my Sanity! Writing about all that was going on, from a Truthful Perspective you see! Since then I have created many! These on my website, you will see! Still creating, writing Poetry, publishing books to help people to see, the current Culling of Humanity and Middle East, Genocide, Catastrophe! Also about Geoengineering where people

were born with eyes, but they cannot see! The constant spraying of our skies, daily! The majority, Brainwashed, Programmed, Hypnotised and Bamboozled, by their own TV!
With
The
Real
Truth,
Being
A
Rare,
Commodity!

Connection!

Do not underestimate the power of connection.

InfusedLights.com

Conspiracy!

Keep your eyes

On your skies

And open your eyes,

They are not CONtrails

As they say on TV!

Although if you

Mention it to

Anybody,

They will say

That you

Are

A

Theorist,

In

Conspiracy!

Constantly!

The Truth,
In coming out,
Always finds
A way!
The explanation
Of the motives,
Behind the
False Flag,
Middle east,
Incursion
On October 7th,
Leading to the
Carpet bombing
And
Genocide,
Taking place
Today!
Ethic cleansing,
Some do say!
Collective
Punishment,
Tribal,
Religious and
Racial hatred,
Along with
Vengance,
Seems to be,
The way!
A land grab,
Undoubtedly!
As time will tell
And we,
Shall see!
With plans to
Drill for gas,
Offshore
And lay a
Pipeline to
Europe,
Below the
Mediterranean Sea!

Ending in
Italy!
"We have a right
To defend ourselves!"
Being the mantra,
Used
Currently!
Also plans
To dig a new
Canal,
Through
Expropriated
Territory,
By using
520 nuclear
Explosions,
To blow
Apart the
Rock,
Undoubtedly!
Bringing in
Billions in
Transit charges,
To the
Oppressors,
Ultimately!
Smoke,
Mirrors,
Lies and
Propaganda,
Having a ring of
Commonality!
As a whole
Community,
Deprived of
Food, water,
Fuel and
Electricity!
Are
Bombed,
Unmercilessly
And
Constantly!

ITALY
GREECE
GREECE-ITALY CONNECTION
TURKEY
CYPRUS
SYRIA
LEBANON
PROPOSED EAST MED PIPELINE
CRETE
ISRAEL-CYPRUS CONNECTION
EGYPT
AGENOR ENERGY
0
100
200 Km

Suez Canal
Israel canal plan
Beirut
بيروت
Damascus
دمشق
Haifa
WEST B
Jerusalem
Alexandria
الإسكندرية
Jordan
Israel
Cairo
القاهرة
New Cairo City
مدينة القاهرة الجديدة
Aqaba
العقبة
Altubaiq Natural Reserve
محمية الطبيق
Al Khanafah Wildlife Sanctuary
محمية الخنفة
Tabuk
تبوك
Sharm El-Sheikh
شرم الشيخ
Hurghada
الغردقة
Asyut
أسيوط

Constipated!

My works laptop
Was really
Slugish!
I was getting
Frustrated!
When
"Your
RAM
Might be
Full up?"
My workmate
Richard
Stated,
So this morning,
I have been
Clearing out
And deleting,
All the
Previous
Revisions,
As due to
The Laptop,
Storing
All
That
Old
Shit!
It was
Obviously,
Constipated!

Constipation

CONtrails!

Wull Boyle:
Look up at the skies...can any of you honestly say this was the Skies you grew up with...😕

I for one do not..I remember good summers and good winter's with storms that brewed up then past leaving clear "Blue" Skies and crisp cold days with sun which was orange back then not white like 90%of the time today...

Almost always complete grey Dome these days and nobody noticing.....

It's Geo-engineering on a Grand Scale....

But hey what do I know right....

But don't worry the Fitba and bookies will keep you from noticing or looking up...

BTW their goal is to have complete Sun Block 365 by 2030.

And incase you didn't know every living organism on the planet needs Sun to live...let that sink in...

Yes that's right I do my homework/research...

David:
They are to busy watching TV and believing all it's tales! They also believe that these long white spreading streaks in the sky, are only CONtrails!

Control Of Humanity!

Viola Solo:
Some of us seen it from the start.

David:
Viola Solo the big move came on the 23rd of March 2020! When we were self imprisoned in our own homes, the majority, stuck inside, in front of the TV! Exactly, where they were, wanted to be, by those, in Authority! To ramp up the fear, against C_V_D! Death statistics, rising cases, in charts, graphs and statistics, getting Brainwashed, Programmed and Hypnotised easily! "We need a Vaxxine, urgently!" Was the cry to the makers of Pharmacy! Who went on to make profits, grotesquely! With complete, global immunity! Oor Bill funded the seven main makers and profited stratospherically! Millions now, no more of them do you see! They are now in either the Crematorium or Cemetery? Prematurely! Billions of others, lives ruined, totally and permanently! To get the Vax injured payout, you have to have a score of percentage points of Disability, of Sixty! New medical conditions like SADS!* Appearing suddenly! Athletes, Sportsmen and the public and Singers, dropping dead, Suddenly! Some Shaking, Violently! Why? "The Doctors are Baffled!" Apparently! Them pocketing the money! Giving jabs, is a lucrative income, obviously! Underway currently, is a Culling of Humanity! Our air being poisoned by soft metallic nano particles of Aluminium, Barium and Strontium from Coal Fly Ash, Graphene oxide and other things, look up the Geoengineering patents and you will see!
The long white spreading streaks in the skies, not even noticed, by the Majority! "They are only CONtrails!" They all agree! Spreading into chemical clouds, blocking our God given Sunshine, depriving us, of making Vitamin D! Leaving us with lowered immune systems, so necessary!

60GHz mm Microwave technology, installed speedily! During lockdown at night! Sneakily! Everywhere now buzzing, especially ears! In each SMART City! Gone already, is our Privacy! All SMART devices spying on you, eternally! Facial recognition, also Reality! Illegal immigrants given four star accommodation, for free! While our own countrymen and women, sleep in cold alleyways, begging for change and pity! A sudden war, by Proxy! Laundering tax payers money, to the bank accounts, of the arms manufacturers, making them, very happy! Taking the populations attention away from the now successful PLANNEDemic, SCAMMEDemic, Emergency!
Now funding Genocide in the Middle East also by Proxy! Cash soon to be, cancelled, permanently, to be, replaced by CBDC**
With a Social Credit System, Programmable Digital money and Vax ID! Living in a fifteen minute City! With LEZs*** with fines, for breaking the rules, accordingly! The New World Order that George Bush Snr spoke about, is in action nowadays obviously! For complete CONTROL of Humanity!

Cough!

Three
Young guys
Tried to
Jump the
Queue!
At
Oran mor,
In Glasgow,
That is the
Wrong thing,
To do!
"What do you
Think that
You are doing?"
An elderly lady
In a red coat,
Did say!
"This is
Glasgow
Pal,
It doesn't
Work
That way!"
He was
Surprised,
A bit
Of a
Toff!
Then
I told him
"She was
Very nice
To you,
She
Could
Have
Just
Told
You,
To

Fu,
Cough!"

Currently!

David:

It's great over here!

It's like an African Climate,

If I was in Scotland just now,

I would be wearing my

Thermal gear!

Millicent:

Oh thats good.

Is Scotland not affected by climate change?

David:

Aye it is most

Definately!

But caused

Mainly,

By the

Long white streaks

In our skies,

That we see

Daily!

Them

Sprayed

Mainly,

By the

Military!

Geoengineering,

SAI,

Strategic

Aerosol

Injection,

Duck Duck Go

These terms,

Then you

Will see,

How our air,

Is being

Poisoned by

Metallic

Nano particles,

(Coal Fly Ash)

Consiisting of

Aluminium,

Barium

And

Strontium,

Mainly!

Which then get

Affected by

EMFs

Electro

Magnetic

Frequency!

Switched on

Deliberately!

They then

Spread out into a

Chemical Silver Grey

Chemical

Blanket,

Then

No more of

The Sun,

Do we see!

We inhale these

Nano Particles,

Easily!

Altzheimer's and

Dementia deaths,

Rising

Stratospherically!

The number one

Killer in the

UK now,

Apparently!

I have written

Two books on this

Subject

Already!

They are

Geoengineering

Poetry and Photos,

Vols 1 and 2!

Working on

Number

Three!

They are

Available on

Amazon,

As

Kindle

And

Paperback,

So please

Check them out

And you

Will

See!

An

Enviromental

Disaster,

That is

Happening,

Globally

And

Currently!

Dance Choreographers Required!

Getting ready for the next PLANNEDemic!

Dark Eventually!

Minx Millar:
May this come to an END my beautiful friend David - get that stone ready and make sure when you aim its OVER.

David
I am going to get a Slingshot.
To help physically, in case Goliath, I see! To aid like the aim of the Truth, in my Poetry! To help open eyes, that do not see! The Absolute Hypocrisy and double standards by those in Authority! Who allow our Air to be Poisoned, daily! Who want to lock us, in a SMART CITY! With a Digital ID, a Crypto wallet for your Programmable CBDC! Social Credit System and Vaxx ID! Facial recognition already, Reality! Gone now is Privacy! With all SMART Appliances, spying on you Constantly! Taking instructions from the Tele Screens as George Orwell in his book 1984 did forsee!
Weather warfare carried out secretly! With many a hostile country, after earthquake, wildfire, hurricane, flood, drought, or Tsunami? Left devastated, wondering, did this

happen, naturally? Soon in the skies, we will see, an alien invasion, supposedly! Utilising all the latest Technology! Including drones controlled by AI, spectacularly! The return of Jesus, they might make you believe, what you think that you see? Sacrificing women and children, to their evil entity! Using them sexually and in slavery! Such dark deeds going on presently! But Hope is ever present as long as life, is still a viability! God exists as does Spirituality! Light always triumphs over dark, Eventually!

Dave Caird!

Day's

Emily Rose Eyre
David Nicoll
Yes I didn't drive a car till I was 50…bcs I didn't need to..I walked or cycled everywhere. I couldn't anymore since around 2010…bcs of all the Thick spraying.

We had to move out of the city in 2016…we were actually forced out by buy to let landlords desperate to buy our house as we were in their way.
Now I'm glad as I've worked on myself… so don't need the inhaler anymore.
I'm glad apart from now being miles away from my elderly parents and all of my family and friends that is. Oh well. Have the machines. That makes up for Human Contact yeah lol 🧕😔

David:
The cities
Get blasted
By both
Geoengineering
Spray's
And
Electro
Magnetic
Ray's!
Both
Done,
To
Shorten
Our
Day's.

Degree's!

Having a
Bit of a
Heat
Wave
Here in
Glasgow,
In

January!
"Last
Week
It wis
Freezin!
Ah wiz
Shakin,
Ma
Knees!
But
Noo,
It's
Eight
Degree's!"

Dick?

This is a

Blow up

Sex Doll,

With a

Difference,

His name is

Mick!

Just

Wondering,

"Does

He

Also

Have,

A

Blow up,

Inflatable,

Dick?"

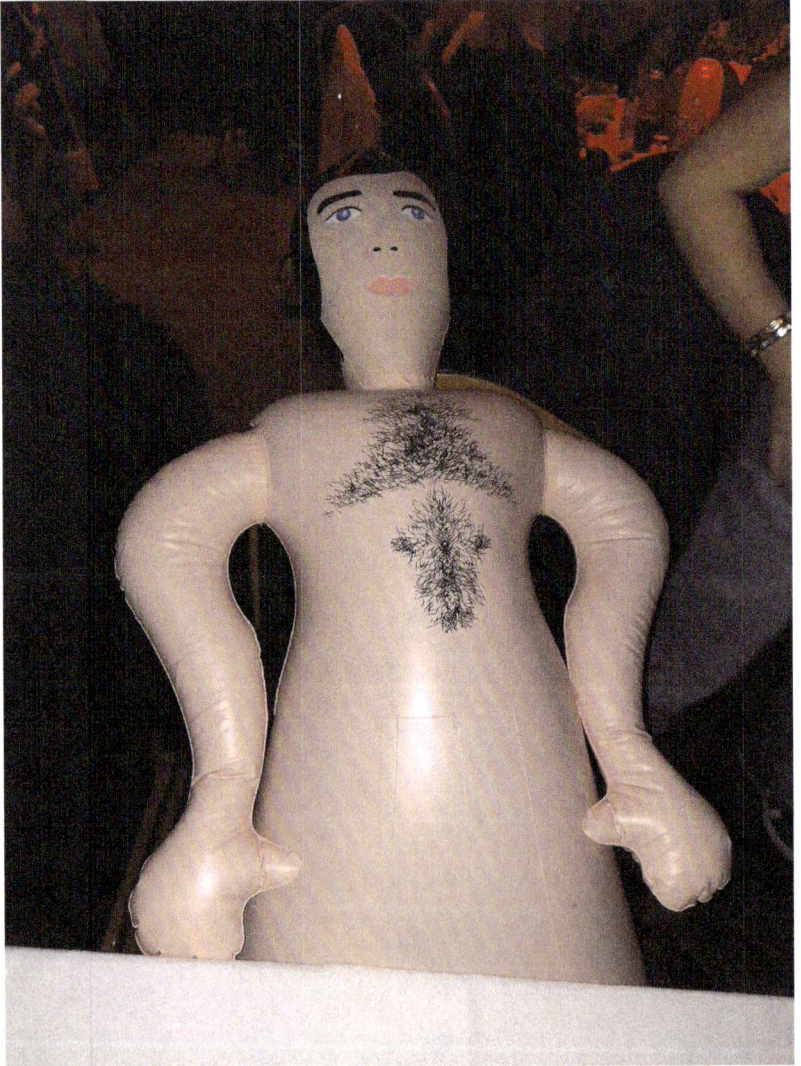

Did You?

Died!

Got talking
To Susan
Who is a nurse
In a care home,
With 130 beds,
Where many
Old sick people,
Lay down
Their heads!
Met her
Sitting outside
Avant Garde,
In Glasgow,
A fine place
To socialise
And
Play!
This
Is what
She had
To say!
We lost
Twenty three,
To
C_V_D!
And
Twenty,
To
DNRs!
These people
Are gone now,
Deceased,
No more
Socialising,
Under
The
Stars!
Couldn't
Get enough,
Body bags!

Or
Ventilators?
It was a drag!
They were
Susceptible,
To
Pulmonary
Infections,
Many of them,
A
Gem!
Any
Respiratory
Issues,
We put
A
DNR!
On
Them!
All the staff
Caught
C_V_D!
They were
Off sick,
At work,
It was
Agony!
With
118 beds full,
Out of
130!
The had
Breathlessness,
Lack of smell,
Oxegen
Levels
Low!
Suffocating
Slowly,
This is true
You dont know,
What that does
To you!
They couldn't

Breathe,
Nothing we did
Would help,
Just had to watch,
Them slip
Away!
These memories
Still haunt me,
To this
Day!
Now
One year later,
Since the time,
I
Cried!
We have
Seventy eight,
Old folk left,
The
Rest,
Have
Died!

Do!

"I watch what I eat!"

"Oh,
You do.
Me too!"

"I stare
At it
Intently,
Then
Eat it ,
As
Quickly,
As
I

Can
Do!"

Do I!

"I don't have
A boyfriend"
The young lady
Did sigh!
Then I
Told her,
"Neither
Do I!'

Doc McLean:

You are a prolific old bugger, Dave.

Hope you are doing well!

Congrats on keeping the wheels turning.

Thanks Doc!

Don't Hate!

Don't hate people for being unvaccinated.

THEY WERE BORN THAT WAY.

Easily!

Leanne Costa:
Some refuse to see even when shown, let's be honest, it's confronting. You every inch of faith in your government and you realise we are at war. People are happier believing in unicorns and rainbows. David Nicoll, I was reading that you discovered the chemos clouds way back and my heart was sore for you. I only saw them a year ago. They do spoil my days!!

David:
Leanne Costa it's better to know, that not to know! It's just trying to convince others is not easy. As you, no doubt know! "They are only CONtrails!' Is the usual flow! The gardeners wondering, why their vegetables are slow, to grow? Sunshine now, a Rarity! Without Criss cross lines in front of it, until they spread out, then no more of the Sun, do you see! Lowering the immune systems in Humanity! By depriving us of Sunshine, to make Vitamin D, inside our body! Slow Poisoning us, with soft metals in nano particulate format, which in Scottish means, Really, Really, Wee! Getting breathed in easily!

Enough!

"How old
Is she?"
Well that
Answer
Is tough!
"She is
The
Same
Age
As
You,
Old
Enough!"

Even On Me?

David:
Karma will kick his Ass.

Lawrence:
For sure 🙏
Just let it go 🌀 🌀

David:
Wiser but poorer
As you can now see!
Lessons are often Costly!
But expose his duplicity,
So that others can see,
The next thing,
He will try his Con
On others and
Possibly,
Even on me?

Every Day!

A child trafficking man
Was heard to say!
Coke you only sell once!
But these kids,
You can sell and
Rent out every day!

Exactly!

There is a

Distinct

Correlation,

Between the

Installation of

Five Gee

And those

Suffering,

From

C_V_D!

Radiation

Poisoning,

Has the

Same

Symptoms,

Exactly!

Fairy!

The EU
Have just
Announced,
That they
Are going to
Implement the
Digital ID!
With a
Digital,
Identity!
And
Digital
Wallet
To
Store,
Your
Programmable,
CBDC!
Central
Bank
Digital
Currency!
Then
Surely,
Cash!
Will be
Cancelled
Very,
Shortly!
Over a
Weekend,
Or on a
Bank holiday?
I heard
Previously!
Sure to create
Pandemonium,
In many
Markets and
In the
Tourist

Entertainment,
Industry!
The
New
World
Order!
Is based on
Technology!
Graphine Oxide
With self forming
Carbon
Nano tubes,
In veins,
Creating
Blood Clots,
Strokes,
Heart Attacks
And
Death,
Ultimately!
The
Morticians,
Pull them
Out of
Cadavers
Veins,
In the
Mortuary!
When
Performing an
Autopsy!
It's turned on
By
Frequency!
From the
Recently
Hastily,
Suddenly,
Secretly,
Installed
Masts and
Square
Lamposts,
With top mounted,

Transmitter
And
Blue
LED!
Operating
Five Gee!
Silently!
60GHz mm
Microwave
Frequency!
With differing
Modulation,
Pulsation,
And
Directed
Energy!
SMART
Meters
And all
SMART
Appliances,
Transmitting and
Receiving
Constantly!
Spying on you,
Unendingly!
Depriving you
Of any,
Privacy!
Introducing
The
Jabbed,
Into the
IOT!
Also
Now
Receivers
And
Transmitters
Unknowingly!
Facial
Recognition
Already,
In many

A
SMART
City!
Like
Glasgow,
Unfortunately!
We were
Self imprisoned
In our own homes,
For what seemed like
An Eternity!
Because of a
Fear based
Propaganda
Exercise,
Pulled off,
Globally!
And on TV
Bill (God) Gates
And Klaus,
From the WEF!
Appeared on TV!
"No one is
Safe until
Everyone's
Been
Jabbed!"
A popular
Decree!
"You will
Own
Nothing,
But be,
Happy!"
The same
Two people,
Exactly!
That held
Event 201,
Just prior to the
Outbreak of
The
PLANNEDemic,
SCAMMEDemic,

Emergency!
The
Majority,
Programmed,
Brainwashed,
Hypnotised and
Bamboozled,
By their
Own TV!
Our children
Now getting
Taught a
Curriculum of
LBGT!
Facilitating
A new
Sex Change,
Industry!
Getting
Groomed for
Paedophilles in
Authority!
After they
Cancel
Cash,
How will
Any child
Get a
Visit,
From
The
Tooth,
Fairy?

Fall!

You
Need to
Stand,
Straight
And
Tall!
But
Pride!
Comes,
Just
Before,
A
Fall!

Fear!

This thought does not bring them much cheer! The Illegal Immigrants get 4 Star free accommodation, but The Truth has nothing to Fear!

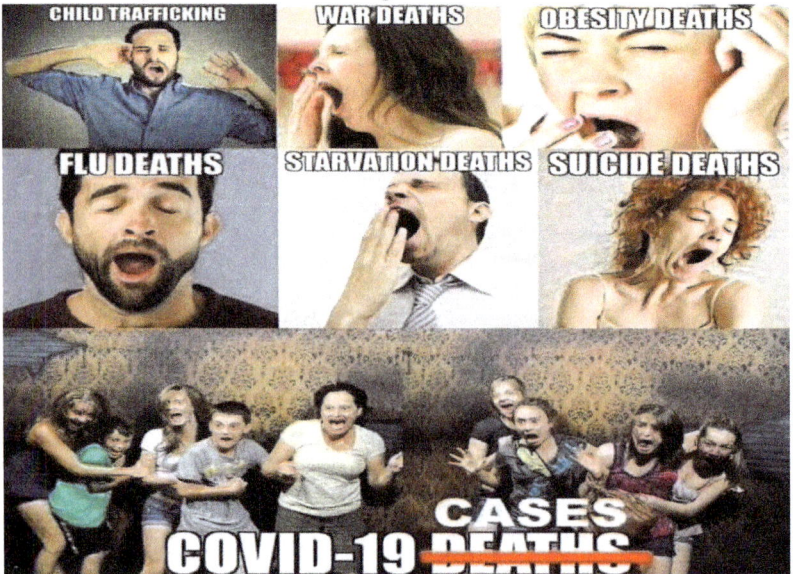

First!

Leanne Costa:

I take this daily,

Add in Apple Cider.

David:

I don't

Drink water

To quench my

Thirst!

Unless

It has been

Passed ,

Through an

Apple Tree,

 First!

BORON MINERAL
ONLY KNOWN NANOBOT REPLICATION INHIBITOR

B O R O N

20 MULE TEAM BORAX — DETERGENT BOOSTER

This mineral intentionally depleted from agricultural process.

BORAX: 1 pinch in 1 pint of distilled water 3 times a day

FDA max dose:
1/8 teaspoon per 100 lbs body weight.
1/4 teaspoon per 200 lbs body weight.

NANO DETOX BATH:
1 Cup Baking Soda
1 Cup Epsom Salt
1 Cup 20 Mule Team Borax
1 Cup Pink Himalayan Sea Salt
   or Redman's Salt.
NEVER use white depleted-minerals
   table salt for any reason.
SOAK AS LONG AS YOU CAN.

Candida is an always-present fungus in the human body there to help decompose the body after death. Many suffer from it's overgrowth:

COMMON CANDIDA SYMPTOMS:

Fatigue	Thrush
Brain fog	Joint pain
Digestive issues	Mild depression
Sinus infections	Urinary tract infections
Recurring yeast infection	Other fungal infections.

BORAX detoxes Fluoride from your body and brain. Raises your pH level from acid to alkaline. Cancer/Candida/Fungus/Nanobots cannot survive in a high alkaline pH environment.

BENEFITS:
Arthritis
Hormone Balance
Decalcify Pineal Gland
Improved Cell Function
Absorption of Minerals
Improved Wound Healing
Encourages Proper pH:
(Cancer can't live in an alkaline environment)
Healthy Blood Sugar
Detoxifies the Liver
Helps the Heart

Flags!

Scottishy Daily Express article:

The Saltire, European and the Ukrainian flag should be flown every day from St Andrew's House, with the former two also being flown from Victoria Quay, with various exceptions depending on special days. These include four days when the Rainbow Flag will be utilised which is the start of LGBT History Month, International Day Against Homophobia, Biphobia and Transphobia, Edinburgh Pride and Glasgow Pride.

I

Wonder

Now,

What our

 Proud

Scottish

Ancestor's,

Would

Say?

If they

Read this,

Newspaper

Headine,

Today!

For Sure!

Formation!

New cloud types

Showing up in

Every nation!

Is this the

Cotton wool

Or

Ping Pong

Ball?

Cloud

Formation!

Free!

Momo:

Yeah even the price of being there has

Git ti make ye feel better than paying

Electricity here and ripping you a new arsehole.

David:

The people are

Being reamed,

That much

I can see!

By the

Massive increase

In costs

For gas and

Electricity!

It's a sad and

Crazy fact,

That lots

Do not see!

In the UK now,

Instead of

Being a

Hard

Working

Citizen,

You are

Better off,

Being a

Refugee!

Four Star

Accomocation,

Full board

And lodging,

Including any

Medical costs

And all

For

Free!

© John Nguyen/JNVisuals

Freezing!

Ji Albagubrath:

3 inches of snow in Rutherglen and I seen a guy doon the Main Street wae shorts on. Aye right pal like yir baws irny freezing!

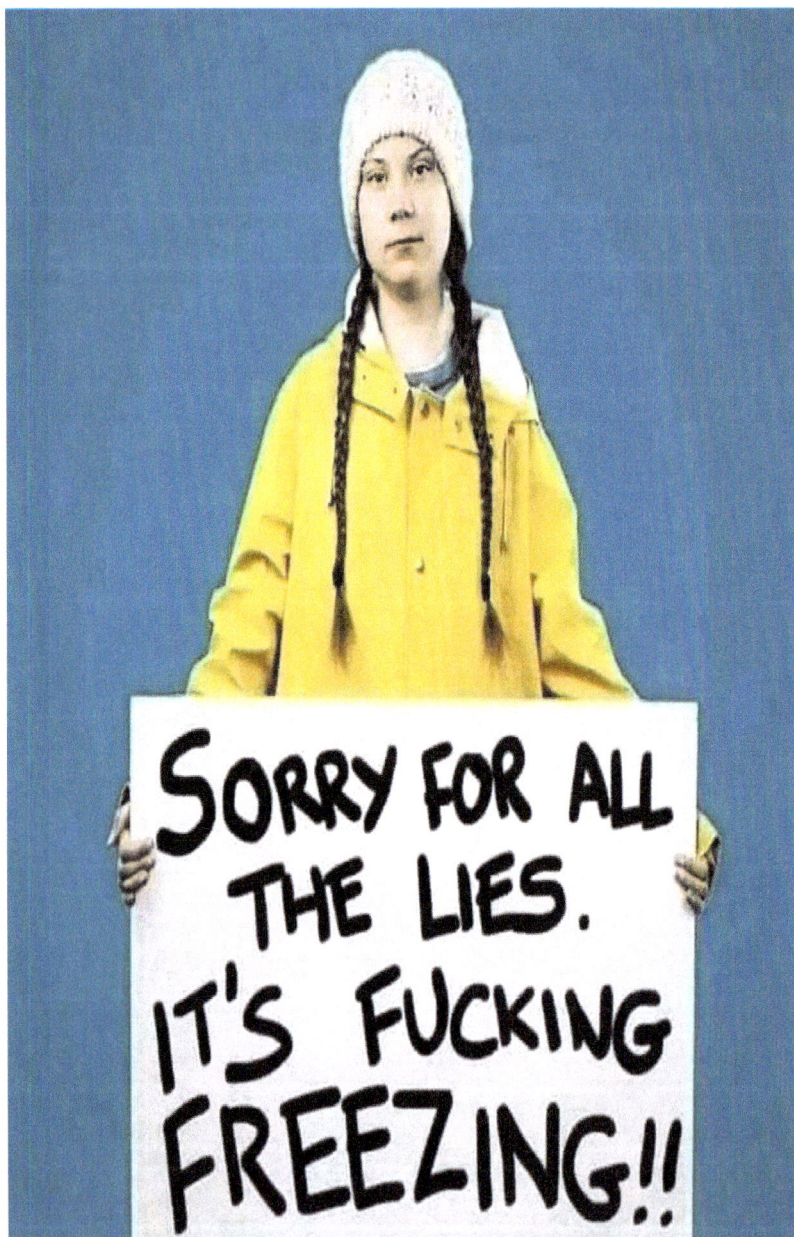

From Me!

Zelda:
Thank you so much for getting into touch.
Sorry for the very late response.
Wonderful to see what you doing.
Keep rising and Shining

David:
Hi Zelda
I have been busy
Producing books
Incorporating
The Truth,
Into my Poetry!
Please check out
My page on
Amazon Author
And my collection,
You will see!
All the best
To you and Rob,
If he is still there?
From me!

Gates!

Comments on dancing doctor's and
Nurses video.

Stuart Denton:
This made me hate medical people as there's nothing professional about any of them. These morons are supposed to save lives but instead they murdered so many people with a fake vaccine for a fake virus and they all knew what they were doing. Sorry if my comment offends anyone, oh wait I don't care if it offends anyone as its easily provable facts.

David:
What about the DNRs and Midazolam and Morphine cocktails for all the elderly?

Stuart:
Yip and the fact they put people on ventilators that didn't need to be on them resulting in people dying from exploded lungs.

David:
There is
Going to be
A lot of
Dancing doctor's,
Nurse's and their
Mate's!
Forming a long
Winding queue,
At the
Pearly
Gate's!

Gay!

What
Strange
Situation,
We have
Today!
When
Women,
Dress
As
Men,
All
Happy
And
Gay!

1924 - 2024
What happened ??

Geoengineered Insanity!

New Cloud

Formations,

Are now in our

Skies!

Never seen before,

But your eyes,

Don't

Tell

Lies!

Yet so few

On the

Beautiful

Earth,

Actually

See!

The

Concocted

Chemically,

Geoengineered

Insanity!

South Africa!

Australia!

Spraying in Action!

Globally!

Just heard a
Breaking
Untold story!
How the
Recently
Attacked country!
Which is now
Raining down bombs,
On civilians,
Women and children,
Mainly!
Has now got
Nuclear bombs,
The size of
Suitcases,
One in
Each of its
Embassy!
In every
Global city!
With the
Message,
"If we get
Invaded,
You will be,
History!"
Is this true?
A
Stranglehold,
From one
Community,
On every
Country,
Globally!

Global Tyranny!

Been cooling it with Ice and did REIKI on myself, so it is healing. Had an interesting situation at the last big one in George square, still to write about it. Not doing my Stand in the park anymore at the moment as the weather is changing. New book in the final stages Scottish Thoughts and Reflections Vol 11! Still working on stuff in the morning's and going to work for 2.30pm until 10pm. Lot of walking, say 15 kms a day, lifting, moving, stacking boxes using trolleys, forklifts and stuff like that, lost so much weight, can no longer be classified as fat! Their must be a moral in that? Sometimes very busy, with thousands of cardboard containers to more, label, stack and store! Speeding through rows of them clipboard in hand, taking some and moving and relabeling, you understand? But Actually it has turned out Beneficially for me! Pays the rent, buys me food, cider and tobacco and I dont have to pay, a Gym fee! Also excercise was never a thought for me! Behind a computer, tablet or laptop screen, mainly! Going down for a smoke once an hour at the flat habitually! Que Sera Sera what will be, will be?
"If it's fir ye,
It'll no go by ye!"
They used to say
In days of
History!
As we
Move
Into
The
Age,
Of
Global
Tyranny!

Glory Be!

Did I
Just
Make,
Some
Scottish,
History?
As I just
Dug up,
Some
Nice
Home
Grown,
Spuds,
In
January!
Glory
Be!

Gone Away!

It's

Estimated!

That the

Rothschild family

Have a net worth of

£500

Trillion!

An

Enormous

Amount,

Even

Today!

But you

Cannot

Take any

With you,

When

Headed,

Through,

The

End

Of

Life's,

Way!

One

Moment

You

Are

Here,

The

Next,

You

Have

Gone,

Away!

Grey!

They sprayed over

Tenerife today!

As the New Year

Holiday makers,

On the

Promenades

And

Beaches

Below,

They

Did

Play!

But no one

Even notices it,

Which is quite

Normal today!

Look how the

Sprayed tails

Dissapate away!

To make a

Blanket

Of

Silver

Grey!

Guilty!

David:
Laura Huber-Kimball
They took this post down,
Which makes me
Sigh!
And ask myself,
Why?
Merely tracks,
Of an
Aircraft's path!
What is the
Mystery?
Unless
It's
A
Conscience,
That
is
Guilty?

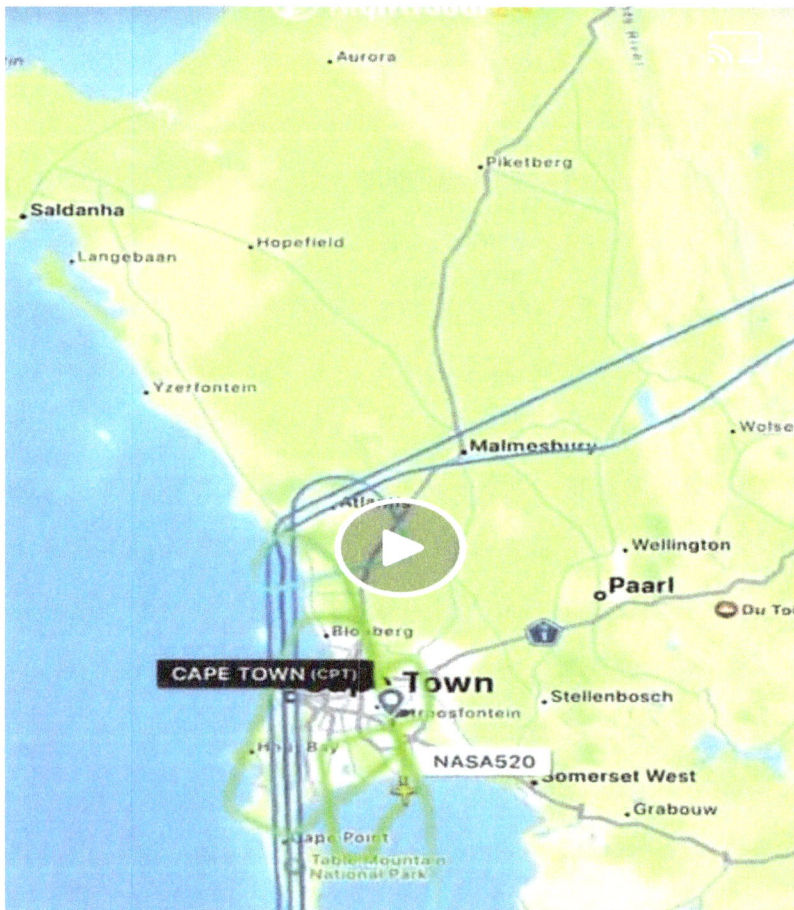

Replying to **Laura Huber-Kimball** · Cancel

Rules

Write a public reply...

Handy!

Ian McKee:
If they use my foreskin to skin graft onto my thumb,
I'll have to start wearing gloves to the poker nights!
I can feel a new poem coming!

David:
It's done
Already!
In one
Fell,
Stroke!
In fact,
It's
Not
A
Poem!
It
Is,
A
POKE!*

* =POetic joKE!

Handy!

That
Sounds
Fine
And
Dandy!
It could
Also be,
Really,
Fuckin
Handy!

Head!

What a

Beautiful

Expression,

To me,

Jade just

Said!

"You

Wake up,

Like a

Cat,

In the

Head!"

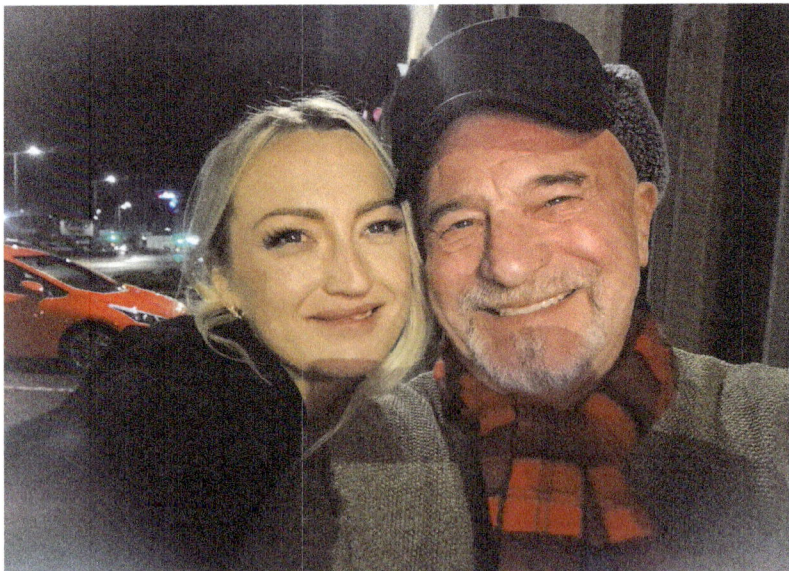

Hi Neale

Message to Neale Hanvey MSP for the Alba Party in Scotland!

I see that you are helping John Watt with his case for the vaxxine injured and thank you for that.
We that is Anti Geoengineering Scotland are going to be holding an Awareness meeting in Edinburgh on Saturday the 16th of March at Mound place from 12 until 3pm.
The purpose of this meeting is to raise Awareness in the Scottish population about the incessant spraying of our skies.
Would you be interested in participating in this event?
I do realise that it is a contentious issue but one that we must face up to as the health of the entire population is at risk here.
I am one of the admin members of SMAAPP Scottish Musicians and Artistes Against the Poisoning of our Planet. The initial reason that this group was formed in 2018 was to raise awareness about the Geoengineering situation.
There are over 160 patents for this with nano particulates including Aluminium, Barium, Strontium, Lithium and Graphene oxide.
Looking forward to hearing from you in due course with best wishes.

Hidden Away!

I moved to
Tenerife,
To try to
Get away,
From the
Glaswegian,
Constant
Geoengineering,
Spray!
But
Today,
Our
Sprayed
Skies here,
Are being
Affected
By
EMFs*
And

Spreading to
A blanket of
Silver
Grey!
The
Sun
Is
Hidden,
Away!

* = Electro Magnetic Frequency!

His Last Trip!

Aldous Huxley, writer of 'Brave New World' asked for LSD on his deathbed. He died hallucinating.

Holly!

When I walked
Out of the Co-op,
In Stornoway,
Just
Yesterday!
There was
A
Young girl,
With
Flowing
Locks,
Holding her
Daddies hand
And
Walking,
My
Way!
"Isn't
She
Beautiful!'
In my
Mind,
To
Myself,
I did
Say!
Then
It
Struck
Me,
It was my
Granddaughter,
Holly!

Xxx

I Replied!

"Do you
Speak
English?"
The
English
Lady,
On
Fanabe
Beach
Promenade
In
Tenerife,
Sighed!
"Aye,
But
With
A
Scottish,
Accent!"
I
Replied!

Immediately!

8.30 pm
"Do you
Want to
Go to the
Shop for me?'
"No!'
"My mother
Would!'
"Well,
Phone
Her then!"
Was the reply,
Immediately!

In 1954!

THE YEAR 1954

WHAT THINGS COST

Average House	£1,863
Pint of Milk	£0.05
Pint of Beer	£0.09
Salary	£420
Litre of Petrol	£0.56
Loaf of Bread	£0.06

UK PRIME MINISTER
Winston Churchill

US PRESIDENT
Dwight D. Eisenhower

World **POPULATION**
2.69 BILLION

UK POPULATION
50.8 MILLION

People born
JACKIE CHAN
ANNIE LENNOX
ANGELA MERKEL
OPRAH WINFREY
DENZEL WASHINGTON
JOHN TRAVOLTA

On Paperback
LORD OF THE FLIES
William Golding

THE FELLOWSHIP OF THE RING (THE LORD OF THE RINGS, #1)
J.R.R. Tolkien

HORTON HEARS A WHO!
Dr. Seuss

I AM LEGEND
Richard Matheson

TWELVE ANGRY MEN
Reginald Rose

1954 Slang

DREAMBOAT – A GOOD LOOKING MALE

PARTY POOPER – SOMEONE WHO ISN'T FUN

COOL CAT – AN INTERESTING OR POPULAR INDIVIDUAL

IN THE NEWS...

11th January
The first weather forecast with an in-vision presenter is televised in the United Kingdom

2nd February
A 27 year old Queen Elizabeth II becomes the only reigning monarch of Australia to have set foot on Australian soil

12th April
Jonas Salk tests his Polio vaccine on 1.6 million children in Canada, Finland and the USA, with encouraging results

21st April
Running Wild on the BBC marks the debut of Morecambe and Wise on British television

6th May
Roger Bannister, a 25-year-old British medical student becomes the first man to run a mile in less than four minutes

4th July
Fourteen years of food rationing in Britain ends when restrictions on the sale and purchase of meat and bacon were lifted

THE US SUPREME COURT RULES THAT STATE-SANCTIONED SEGREGATION OF PUBLIC SCHOOLS IS A VIOLATION OF THE 14TH AMENDMENT AND IS THEREFORE UNCONSTITUTIONAL

WEST BROMWICH ALBION WIN THE FA CUP FINAL FOR THE FOURTH TIME, BEATING PRESTON NORTH END 3-2 IN THE FINAL AT WEMBLEY

'BETTY CROCKER'S GOOD AND EASY COOKBOOK' BECOMES A BEST SELLER AND IS DESCRIBED AS 'AN ENTIRELY NEW KIND OF COOKBOOK, TO HELP HOMEMAKERS SPEED UP THEIR COOKING BY USING CONVENIENCE FOODS'

in style...

Women
POODLE HAIRCUTS
PENCIL SKIRTS
BELTED CLOTH COATS
SWING DRESSES

Men
SIDE PARTED HAIR
TWEED TROUSERS
WOOL CARDIGANS
GINGHAM PRINT SHIRTS

IN FILM...
White Christmas
20,000 Leagues Under the Sea
Gone With The Wind
A Star Is Born
Rear Window
Cinderella

On Television
THE GROVE FAMILY
THE FLOWERPOT MEN
WATCH WITH MOTHER
THE GOOD OLD DAYS
COME DANCING
ZOO QUEST

ON THE RADIO....
Hold My Hand - Don Cornell
Three Coins In The Fountain - Frank Sinatra
Secret Love - Doris Day
I See The Moon - The Stargazers
Little Things Mean a Lot - Kitty Kallen

Inbox!

Colleen McCarthy:
Censored in Canada, cannot be viewed?!!!

David:

Looks like

I am your new

Digital postman,

Due to Trudeau!

With him

Not allowing

You Canadians,

Any news to know!

He is a right Puss!

I wish him the Pox!

To read the article,

Check your

Messenger,

Inbox!

Instead!

Got invited by
Jesse Hal
Of
The Missing Link,
If he could
Interview me?
"Could I please
Send him some
Books of my

Poetry?
Well,
What a
Pleasure,
That
Would be!
So I
Contacted,
A
Courier,
Known as
DPD!
To deliver a
Package,
Containing
Four books,
To Jesse!
First,
They didn't
Collect it,
Until
Appointment
Pick up day,
Number
Three!
Then it was
On its way,
Eventually!
To
Calgary!
It's now
Over a
Month later,
A
Thought
Came to
My
Head!
"I
Should
Have
Used,
Carrier

Pigeon's,
Instead!

Irish Border!

PLEASE
CLOSE
GATE

Is Happy!

Ian McKee:
He's no liking this cold weather 🥶

David:
Are you?

Ian:
I want to be back in the reef.
Is your couch available?

David:
Only one wee
Technicality!
Both Momo
And my
Oldest son
Are still to
Visit me,
With neither
Having confirmed,
What dates
That them,
I will see!
Once they have
Confirmed
Their plans,
Then in the
Gaps,
We could see?
The couch is
Pretty short
Though,
Unless you cut
Your legs off,
Below the
Knee?
Do you now
Fancy
A

Hot Oil
Massage?
With an
Ending,
That is
Happy!

Is Tae Me!

The Scotia bar, Glasgow.

This is my favourite bar in the
Whole of Scotland,
It has lots of style and grace!
It's an amazing live music venue
And poetic place!
First opened in the year of 1792
And still going strong!
From the Glasgow Literary Lounge
To Kinfolk, on Thursday evenings,
Where everyone plays
And sings along!
Lot's of friendly people to meet,
Many who perform incredibly
With guitars and vocals,
So strong!
It's like being inside an old
Wooden ship as you will see!
For incredible Rock N Roll,
See Jeff Jeffrey!
Rab and the Rabble Rousers
Also brilliant, play occasionally!
The best live acts, undoubtedly!
Bar staff that are friendly!
Please vote for the Scotia
As the best pub in
Scotland this year,
Because it
Certainly
Is Tae Me!

Posts   About   More ▾

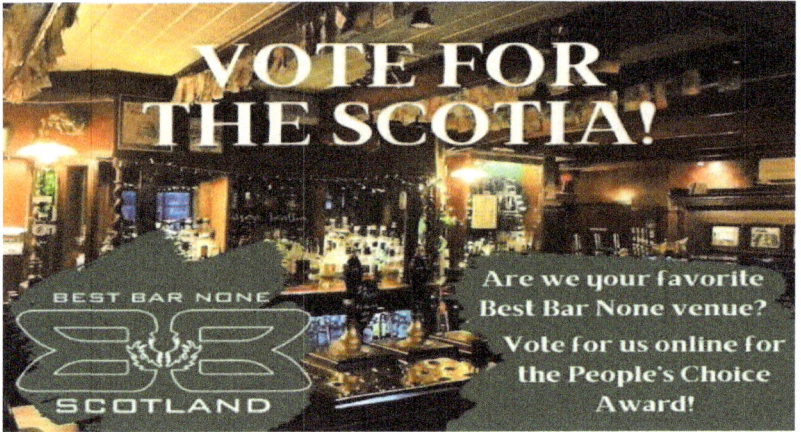

👍❤️ 108   67 comments · 11 shares

❤️ Love   💬 Comment   ↗ Share

 **The Scotia**
6 d · 🌐

Calling all eggheads & dregheads!
On Sunday 22nd Of October,
for £1 per person to ch... See more

SCOTIA BAR
MUSIC QUIZ

It Again!

A wee poke about it!...Again!...Ended up in a very strange situation today as Scotland against SA did play,to show i was unbiased and didnt care who would lose a very unique combination of clothes i did choose! With Springbok strip on top, a South African supporter all would know finished off with a Royal Stewart tartan kilt below! When it got to 21 nil, I could hardly look and promptly posted "I am a Bok supporter!" on Face book! Must be honest, it did cause strain and with such a dismal performance from my homeland team, in no rush to experience it again!

It!

Listening to

Table side chatter

Can be so

Full of

Wit!

Like

Paul and

Louise's

Conversation,

"Men don't see

All the job's to do,

When it comes

To

Housework!"

"Oh we do!"

"So

Do you,

Just

Fk*n

Ignore

It?"

Ity!

On the
Loch Seaforth ferry
From Ullapool to
Stornoway!
To see my children
And grandchildren
To
Laugh,
Love
And
Play!
Then a
Bell
Goes off,
"We are doing
Our
Fire drill
Today!"
Then
People in
Yellow vests,
Red and white
Helmets,
Taking
Muster,
The hand radio
Sounding
Away!
As the ferry
Lurches slowly,
From side
To side!
Outside

It's
Dark,
Cold
Wet
And
Windy!
As we all
Continue,
On our
Way!
Heading back
To my
Birthplace!
Once more!
Great times,
Lie in
Store!
Old
Friends
And
Family!
All to
See!
With an
Occasion
On the
12th of
February!
Where it
Will be,
My Three
Score years
And Tenth,
Rotation
Of the
Sun,
On
My
Life's,
Journey!
Grateful
For a
Beautiful
Family,

Who are all
Happy
And
Healthy!
Grateful
For a
Life of
Much
Adventure,
Travel,
Excitement
Music
Mass
Djembe,
Drumming
With
Poetry!
As US
(United Souls)
And
Hakuna
Matata,
Creating
Lasting
Audible
Memory!
Harmonising,
Living
Free!
Grateful
For visiting
Places in
Africa
Like the
Masa
Mara,
Serengeti
And
Ngorogoro
Crater,
That I used
To see,
As a child
In nature

Programmes,
On the
TV!
Grateful
For a
Life
Full
Of
Passion
And
Creation,
Whether
Building a
Tree house,
Earthship,
And
Meditating
In a
Hammock,
Hung
Between
Palm
Tree!
Grateful
For an
Alternative
Life in
Tenerife,
Costa
Adeje!
Grateful
For
Hybrid
Working
And
Digital
Nomad,
Ity!

Jokingly!

The new
Massage and
Foot Spa,
Has opened just
Recently!
On the beach
Called
Fanabe!
But the
Fish tanks,
Are still
Empty!
Of the
Flesh
Eating
Fish!
Which
Are so
Necessary!
To eat the
Skin flakes,
From your
Feet,
So
Easily!
Asked
Alex,
The
Owner,
"Are
They
Pirhannas?'*
Jokingly!

*=Famous South American flesh eating fish.

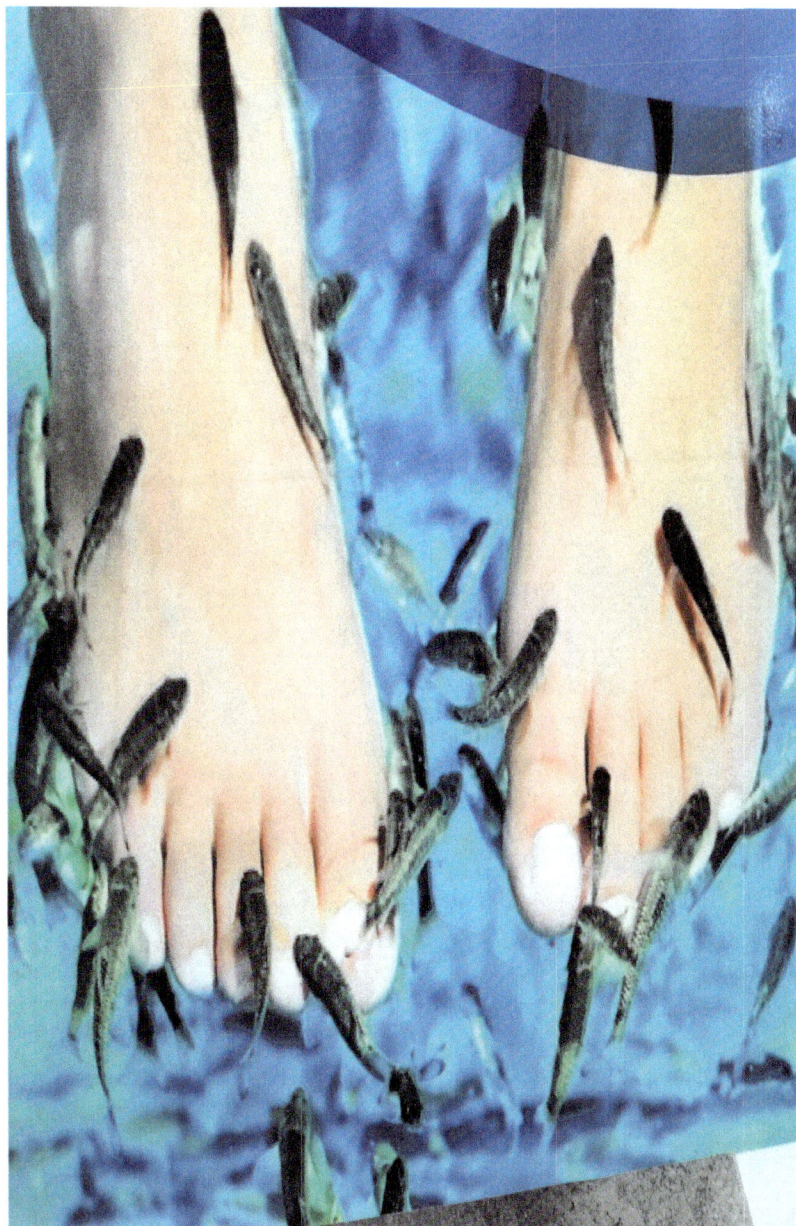

Jubilee!

Tore Nyrud:
It is the same all over.
Until the spraying stops
I know the wrong forces
Are still at the rudder.

David:
It was
Quite amazing,
As one day,
I did see!
No long white
Spreading Streaks
In the sky,
Anywhere
To see!
A real,
Rarity!
Blue skies,
As it used
To be!
Mentioned it
To my friend,
Standing next to the
Firth to Forth,
Canal in Glasgow,
"Why should this be?
We get
Sprayed,
Constantly
And
Daily!"
He then
Told me,
"Today,
Is
The
Queens,
Jubilee!"

Just Wait And See!

News Report, December 2023

The extent of hunger in Gaza has eclipsed even the near-famines in Afghanistan and Yemen of recent years, according to figures in the report.

'Everybody in Gaza is hungry'

"It doesn't get any worse," the World Food Programme's chief economist, Arif Husain, said.

"I have never seen something at the scale that is happening in Gaza and at this speed – how quickly it has happened in just a matter of two months."

The report by 23 UN and nongovernmental agencies found that the entire population in Gaza is in a food crisis with 576,600 people at catastrophic – or starvation – levels.

"It is a situation where pretty much everybody in Gaza is hungry," Husain said.

"People are very, very close to large outbreaks of disease because their immune systems have become so weak because they don't have enough nourishment," he said.

The situation is

Catastrophic!

Undoubtedly!

Set up,

In my

Opinion,

Deliberately!

The event on the

Seventh of October,

2023!

Has many

Questions

For me!

Like

Where did

Hama's get

Motorised

Hang gliders from?

As they do not

Have any!

And what plane,

Did the

Paratroopers

Jump from?

There are

No Airstrips,

In the enclosure,

Funnily!

Before creating

Carnage on

The ground,

At the festival,

Frequented by

Many!

Then

Helicopter

Gunships arrive,

Blowing up cars

In the melee!

When the fence

Was breached,

Where were

The

Iserali

Air force

And

Army?

On a

Seven hour

Stand down,

Apparently!

Innocent

Men, women

And children,

Killed

Prematurely!

Tanks blowing up

Houses in a

Kibbutz,

Killing their

Own people,

Obviously!

A

False Flag

Operation,

Quite

Possibly?

Hostages taken

Who were

Once free!

Then the

MSM and TV!

Telling many a

Story!

Of many a

Decapitated,

Baby!

Misinformation,

Disinformation

And

Propaganda,

Apparently!

"We

Have a

Right to

Defend,

Ourselves!"

Repeated by

All the

Global leader's,

Daily!

Then the

Bombing started

With DUMB

And

SMART bomb's,

Killing an

Innocent population,

Devestatingly!

Living in an

Open air

Concentration camp!

Eternally!

Squashed into

Gazza from the

Clearing of

Palesine,

In the Nakba,

Seventy

Years,

Previously!

Now many

Have been

Prisoners,

Since being a

Baby!

The

Constant

Bombardment

Now heading,

For the

Equivalnent,

In

Explosive power

Of

Hiroshima,

Times

Three!

The population

Deprived of

Food, water,

Gas and

Electricity!

Starvation,

Disease

And

Dysentry!

Will decimate

Their numbers

Undoubtedly!

While the

Western world,

Look on,

Supplying

Financial aid,

And all things

Military!

It will

Come back and

Bite them

In their

Ass,

Ultimately!

Grotesque photos

Of injured children

And bombed out

Neighborhoods

Appearing daily!

On every

Global TV!

Billion's

Protesting and

Marching,

In

Solidarity!

A

Land

Grab!

It is,

Undoubtedly!

As a

Massive Gas field,

Has been found off

Gazza,

And a pipeline to

Europe,

Planned

Already!

Going under the

Mediteranean Sea!

Landing in

Italy!

Hence the

Silence,

Of the

Atrocity!

Zionism

Now wrapping its

Tentacles,

Globally!

With a

Percentage of

Eighty!

Holding dual

Nationality,

In the US

Congress,

Currently!

Also plans

For the

Ben Gurion canal,

Going through

Northern

Gazza,

Instead of the

Suez canal,

This is

Plan B!

A distinct

Possibility,

Of a

Furtherance

Of

Hostility!

Ending in

World

War

Three!

Ultimately!

Will these

Things

Happen?

Lets

Just

Wait

And

See!

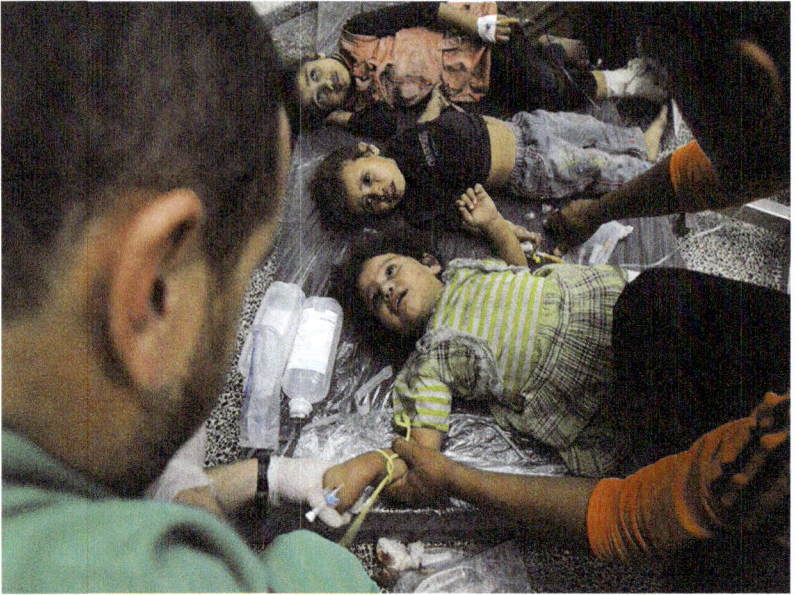

Kidding!

Chris Hoeta:
Polititions are self entitled clowns and desperately need reviewing or a good bashing.

David:
They are
Mere puppets
Doing their master's
Bidding!
Receiving kickbacks/
Bribes through
"Lobbying"
And when
Confronted
With this,
Say
"Are
You
Kidding?"

Knee!

When it
Comes
To post
Jab deaths,
Or
Severe
Permanent
Physical
Disability?
The doctors
Are all
Baffled
Apparently!
Which
Is the
Correct
Word,

Exactly!
To
Silence
An
Exhaust ,
You
Baffle it!
In this case
They were
Baffled,
By
Money!
Supplied
By the
Many,
Pharmaceutical
Company!
Getting paid
For jabbing
One and all,
Whether
Young or old?
Sick or
Healthy?
With the
Propaganda of
Safe and
Effective!
Now in
Jeopardy!
As
SADS*
Appears
Suddenly!
People,
Athletes,
Sportsmen,
Actor's
All
Dropping
Dead,
Some

Shaking,
Violently!
Death for
Them,
Came
Quickly!
Millions of
Other's,
Not so
Lucky!
Their lives
Destroyed,
Because they
Took it to
Save
Granny!
Some
Bedridden
Permanently,
A leg
Amputated
Below the
Knee!

No

Positive

Future,

Do they

Forsee!

While the

Makers

Of the mix,

Have

From

Prosecution,

Immunity!

Know!

"Did I get a
Suntan,
On my legs?"
Asked
Momo!
"Is anyone
Going
To see it?
When you
Get back to
Scotland,
In
Winter?"
I wanted
To
Know!

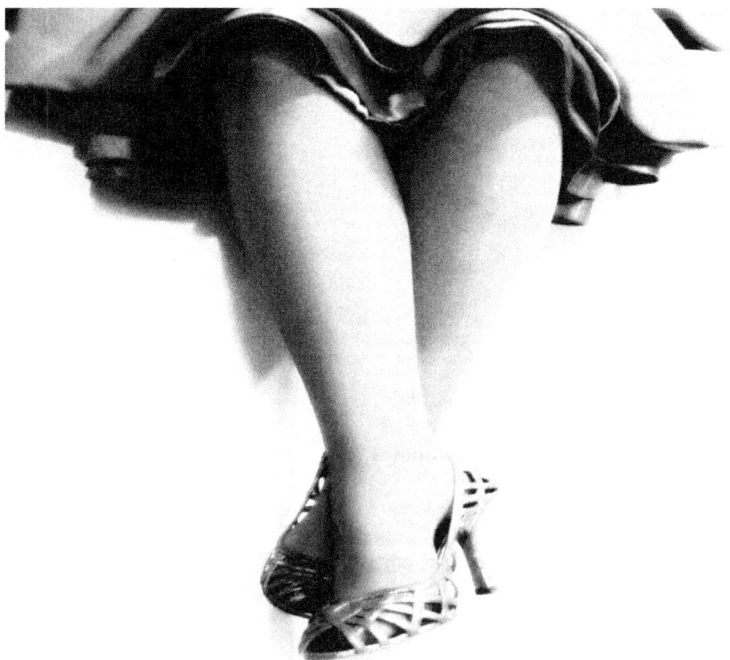

Land One Day!

The abhorrent photos and videos
Of innocent women and children,
Bombed and slaughtered
In the Middle East today!
Leaves billions revolted,
While others are
Happy and gay!
But what would
You say?
If one day,
It is
YOUR
Women
And
Children,
That are
Treated
In this way?
With the
Western world,
Giving
Financial
Backing,
Armament's,
And the
"All OK!"
It will
Come back
To
Haunt them,
In their
Own
Land,
One
Day!

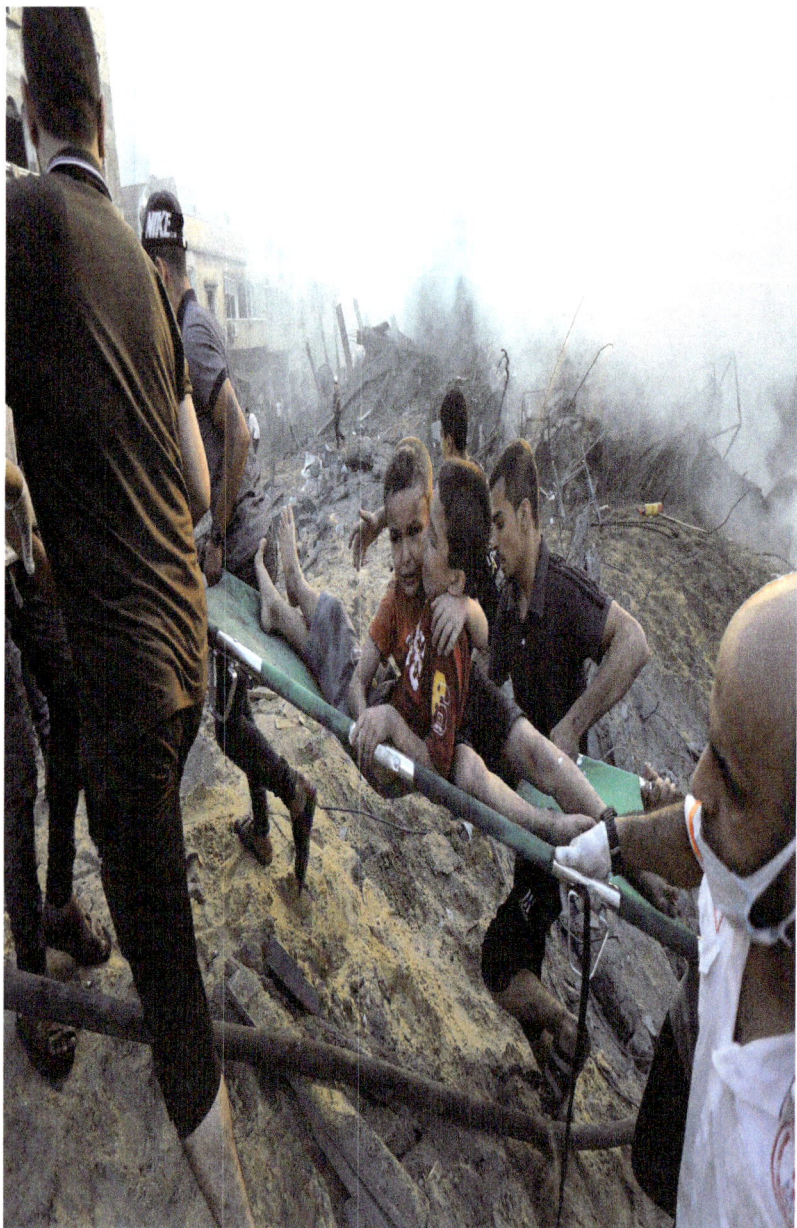

Later!

"What would you
Like to drink?"
I asked while
My neck
Made a
Reach!
"Oohh
I would
Love to have
Sex on the
Beach!"
This was not
Problem,
Being a
Freethinking
Conspirator!
We can
Catch
A taxi,
To the
Beach,
Later!

Laughter To You!

This book contains

Adventure and

Humorous Poetry,

Written and experienced

In a three month stay,

In Costa Adaje!

Covering subjects like

Para Sailing,

Whale Watching

With Galatea sailing,

La Gomera visiting,

Hot Oil massages,

The Strip

And Jet Ski!

Also Scuba Diving

In the crystal blue,

Clear Sea!

David having a

Scottish sense of

Humour and

Ancestry!

Also many

A story,

Of

Performer's

In the

Entertainment,

Industry!

Frankie Mack,

Mister Sister,

Roxy Risque too!

Diane's bar,

Busking,

Da Angelo restaraunt,

Coffee shops and

Skies of

Blue!

With matching

Photographs,

To take

Memories,

Home with you!

It is called

Tenerife Thoughts and Reflections Vol 1

Currently working on Vol 2!

Available on Amazon

And his website

www.davidnicoll.co.uk

To bring

Happy memories

And

Laughter

To You!

Tenerife Thoughts and Reflections Vol 1

David Nicoll

Longer Away!

My pal
Bluebird,
Brought
His
Bird,
Around
Today,
He
Was
Very
Glad,
That
I
Am,
No
Longer,
Away!

Love!

25 million
Nano particles
In every breath,
Toxic soft metals
Enough to scare
You to death!
All
Sprayed
From
Above!
Out of
Malice,
Not
Love!

Mack!

To be Frank
With you,
In good
Crack!
The most
Talented
Frank in
Scotland
And
Tenerife,
Is
Frankie
Mack!

Against
THE ODDS
AN EVENING WITH
FRANKIE MACK

ACCOMPANIED BY HIS SPECTACULAR LIVE SHOWBAND

MAY 04TH

SUPPORTED BY THE KENNEDYS PROJECT & ALSO A SPECIAL GUEST APPEARANCE

SILVER, GOLD & DIAMOND PACKAGES AVAILABLE

ASSEMBLY ROOMS, GEORGE STREET, EDINBURGH

Meant Happy!

We used to watch
Pantomime
And thought
Nothing of it,
Men dressed
As women,
As we
Could see!
That was
In the days,
When
Gay,
Meant
Happy!

Meeeeee!!!!!

Dave John Emoven:
All zeebest...

David:
Having wee
Rose wine,
Yo make me
Feel fine!
As fine
As I
Can be!
Thank you God,
Universal Creator,
To let me reach
The age,
Of
Seventy!
Blessed with a
Beautiful
Healthy,
Family!
And
Just
Sang to
Myself
"Happy
Birthday,
To
Meeeeee!!!!!"

Mercy!

They are doing a land grab! As far as I can see, would like their, relatively, recently, created country! To be Palestinian free! Following an ethic cleansing programme, without any, mercy! With a bloodlust on their hearts and racial tribal hatred, we can see! Armed by the West, moving on from their current War on Proxy! Due to a central command NATO underground bunker headquarters, outside Kiev, being destroyed, completely! That war is now History! All focus on the multi national carrier fleet,in the Mediterranean Sea! To bomb whom? We will soon find out, inevitably! Could this be, the start, or continuation? Of World War Three? Do they want the natural gas reserves, just offshore Gazza? They do, definitely! With plans to run a pipeline to supply Europe, via Italy! A new canal to rival the Suez, is planned already! Running through North Gaza, so they want it Empty! Hence the Genocide, Without Mercy!

Message from Leanne!

David, I have started reading and sadly, I understand and have researched everything you write about. More sad than that my husband will not believe a bar of it. He cannot see the fake skies and does not question the lies. Everyday I pray he will look up and see that we are at war. They do not drop bombs, but chemicals and poisons. It is not easy living with an ostrich.

Military!

David:
Have you got Flightradar24 on your phone?

Dawny Banne:
Yeah!

David:
The planes
Often don't show
As you
No doubt know!
The ones that
You

Don't
See,
Are
Military!

Mind!

BE WHO YOU ARE AND SAY WHAT YOU FEEL, BECAUSE THOSE WHO MIND, DON'T MATTER AND THOSE WHO MATTER, DON'T MIND.

Money!

Laura Huber-Kimball:
Right?!! Sudden Adult Death Syndrome- SADS, a disease NEVER BEFORE seen in human history, coinciding exactly with the mRNA jabs.
Nothing suspicious about THAT, right?!!
Nothin' to see here, folks, move along...   Oh, LOOK! ... a Squirrel!

David:
And the doctors are baffled!

Laura Huber-Kimball:
Rather, they want us to THINK they're baffled!
They are not stupid and neither are we!

David:
For them to say
That they are Baffled,
Is really not Funny!
As instead of choosing
The Hippocratic Oath!
They have been
Silenced,
By
Money!

"Sudden adult death syndrome" sounds so much nicer than GENOCIDE.

My Poetry!

Shaunagh Chapman:
You need to correct
"Contrails" to "Ch*mtrails".

David:
I was being
Sarcastic
You see!
Because
Ch*mtrails,
Is not a term,
Liked by
Those in,
Authority!
They want
Us to
Believe that
It is only,
Condensation trails,
That in our skies,
We see!
But luckily we
Are not as stupid
As that,
Fortunately!
Because real
CONtrails,
Only last for
A short time,
They don't stretch,
As far as the eye
Can see!
Then spread out
Into a chemical haze,
To block the
Sunshine,
That God
Gives us,
For
Free!
We need it

For our
Immune
System,
In the
Creation of
Vitamin D!
If you use
The word
Ch*mtrails,
Facebook
Would ban you,
Immediately!
As they never
Like to let the
Truth out!
Obviously!
In fact
I am
On a
Posting
Ban,
By
Them,
Currently!
For
Weaving
The
Truth,
Into
My
Poetry!

To Me!

The
Thought Police,
(Fact Checkers)
At this will be,
Not very
Happy!
Which brings
Great joy and
Amusement,

To
Me!

Shaunagh Chapman
A wee poem
For you,
In fact,
There
Are
Two!

Name Something!

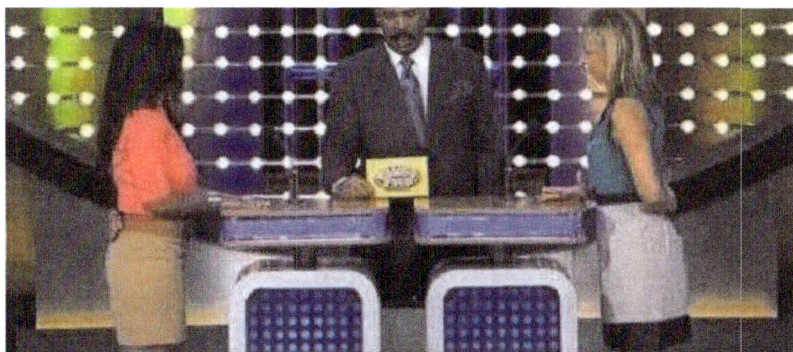

If you enjoyed the book,

Please do a review!

On Amazon,

Facebook,

Or any other

Platforms?

Thank you!

To see my other books,

Please look up my name

On Amazon Author!

Between the

Books and CDs,

There are

Greatfully,

Quiet a Few!

Interesting times

That we live in

Nowadays,

As we all

Can see!

Interesting,

But not,

Funny!

If you

Would like

To do,

A

Review?

Then please

Put it on

Amazon and

Send

It

To

Me!

Marked

Review,

To davidrbnicoll@gmail.com

Have a

Good day

And

Thank You!

Printed in Great Britain
by Amazon